San Francisco by Cable Car

San Francisco by Cable Car

by

George Young

with

Bill Henkin and David Williams

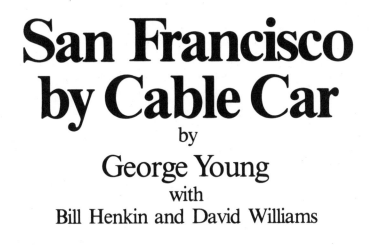

Grateful acknowledgement is made to the following for permission to reprint previously published material:
Excerpt from *Bay Window Bohemia* by Oscar Lewis. Copyright ©1956 by Oscar Lewis. Reprinted by permission of Doubleday & Co., Inc.
Excerpt from *The Barbary Coast: An Informal History of the San Francisco Underworld* by Herbert Ashbury. Copyright ©1933 by Herbert Ashbury. Reprinted by permission of Alfred A. Knopf, Inc.
Excerpt from *The Fantastic City* by Amelia Raysome Neville. Copyright ©1932 by Riverside Press. Reprinted by permission of Houghton Mifflin Company.
Excerpt from *Mission to Metropolis* by Oscar Lewis. Copyright ©1966 by Oscar Lewis. Reprinted by permission of Darwin Publications.
Excerpt from *San Francisco's Golden Era* by Lucius Beebe and Charles Clegg. Copyright ©1960 by Howell-North. Reprinted by permission of Darwin Publications.
Excerpt from *Bohemian San Francisco* by Clarence Edwords. Copyright ©1914. Facsimile reprint by Sillouette Press 1973.

ISBN 0-914728-46-6
First Edition: June 1984

Photo credits: The historical photographs herein were supplied through the kind courtesy of The Bancroft Library & The San Francisco Public Library; all contemporary photographs are by Jim Hutchins; line drawings by Hyla Shifra Bolsta; maps, cover & book design by Bill Yenne; cover photo by Bill Yenne.

TABLE OF CONTENTS

1. Preface: How to Make the Best Use of this Book.   pg. viii

This book is about the Cable Cars and The City whose hills they climb — San Francisco, of course. Although Cables once ran in many other places, including New York, Los Angeles, Seattle, Denver, Chicago, London, and Sydney, Australia, they were first invented in San Francisco and exist nowhere else in the world today. Here and there you can find funicular cars, but their operation is different from that of San Francisco's Cables.

2. The Phoenix of Crysopylae:
   A Brief Introduction to San Francisco's Lore.   pg. 2
3. The Last Magic Carpet: A Brief History of the Cable Cars, Including Explanations of What They Are and How They Work.   pg. 14
4. The Powell - Hyde Line.   pg. 26
   A. Introduction
   B. *Union Square.* San Francisco major shopping district lies immediately adjacent to its largest theatres, and to many of The City's greatest hotels, including the legendary St. Francis.   pg. 33
   C. *Chinatown.* This largest Chinese settlement outside the Orient offers scintillating shopping, pungent history, and some captivating examples of the high art of Chinese culture. *(Also reached on the California Line.)*   pg. 49
   D. *Russian Hill.* Its beautiful scenery and spectacular views made this area an early favorite among San Francisco's first settlers. Home of "the crookedest street in the world," Russian Hill is also full of unexpected parks and walkways, and dotted with pockets of shops, cafes, and art galleries.   pg. 63
   E. *Fisherman's Wharf Area.* Parts of the Wharf still function as they did in the nineteenth century, as the home of The City's local fishing fleets.
   Claimed as the second most popular tourist attraction complex in America, next to Disneyland, its newer features include internationally famous restaurants, souvenir shopping, games, amusements, and tour boats. The Wharf Area includes Ghirardelli Square, The Cannery and Pier 39. *(Also reached via the Powell-Mason Line.)*   pg. 67

5. The Powell - Mason Line.   pg. *78*
   A. Introduction
   B. *North Beach.* One of The City's original Italian settle-
      ments, made famous by the poets, musicians, and artists of the
      Generation, North Beach remains a bastion of Bohemian culture.
      Superb coffee houses and fine restaurants stand side by side with
      unique shopping and sight-seeing opportunities, the Broadway
      night clubs, and some of San Francisco's best-known landmarks,
      such as Coit Tower and Telegraph Hill. *(Chinatown is next to
      North Beach and can also be reached via the Powell-Mason
      Line.)*   pg. *81*
   C. *Maiden Lane.* Just east of Union Square, this two-block-long
      alley houses some of San Francisco's most exclusive shops, a bit
      of embarrassing history, and the only building Frank Lloyd
      Wright ever designed that is not a free-standing structure.   pg. *95*
   D. *Market Street.* Much of San Francisco's most colorful history
      orginated on lower Market Street. Much of its modern history is
      being written in this area's redevelopment, which is marked by
      high-rise architecture, the exemplary restoration of fine, older
      structures, and the classic Palace Hotel, an architectural wonder
      of its day whose grace and charm still seem to transcend time.

6. The California Line.   pg. *110*
   A. *The Embarcadero Center.* San Francisco's easternmost
      business section used to be its produce market. Today, it is nearly a
      model city itself, featuring restaurants, shops, offices, and homes,
      in a complex of buildings surrounded by parks and open space.
      All of this is within easy walking distance from The City's
      Financial District and the Ferry Building, where boats depart on
      a regular schedule for Sausalito, Tiburon, and points north. pg. *113*
   B. *The Old Barbary Coast Area.* Once the embodiment of
      rowdiness and loose living, this section of San Francisco —
      many of whose buildings housed bordellos, opium dens, and the
      headquarters of pirates and thieves — is better - known today as
      home of The City's finest Downtown antique shops and
      decorator salons, *Jackson Square.* It is the only district of
      Downtown San Francisco to have survived the Earthquake and
      Fire of 1906 relatively intact.   pg. *120*

C. *Montgomery Street.* Montgomery Street, the heart of
San Francisco's Financial District, is one of the busiest, wealthiest
business centers in the world. As you might expect in an area
frequented by bankers, brokers, and executives from some of the
world's largest corporations, many of The City's highest-quality
luncheon restaurants are situated in these few square blocks, just
downhill from Chinatown. pg. *128*

D. *Nob Hill.* The highest of San Francisco's downtown hills,
this is where the "Big Four" — Mark Hopkins, Leland Stanford,
Charles Crocker, and Collis P. Huntington — built their
mansions in the days when they derived enormous personal
wealth from the building of the railroads and the mining of the
gold and silver that helped make San Francisco one of the most
alluring cities the world has ever known. Today, luxury hotels,
like the Mark Hopkins and the Fairmont, along with exclusive
apartments, clubs, Grace Cathedral, and three-star dining
establishments, dominate the hill. pg. *139*

E. *Polk Street.* At the end of the California line lies a unique
commercial street where high fashion gets the low-down on street
life. Largely, but by no means exclusively, oriented toward the
City's prominent homophile community, Polk Street has a little
something for everybody, from cheap fast food to fine cuisine of
several nations; from rare antiques and art to the latest fad
among the bubblegum set. pg. *150*

7. Appendices
   A. Places you might want to see on your visit to San
      Francisco that you cannot reach by Cable Car. pg. *152*
   B. Tours and day-trips beyond the San Francisco city limits. pg. *158*
   C. Guided tours of specific San Francisco neighborhoods. pg. *161*
   D. Useful telephone numbers. pg. *165*
   E. Selected bibliography. pg. *170*

PREFACE:
How to Make
the Best Use
of This Book

This book is about the Cable Cars and The City whose hills they climb—San Francisco, of course. Although Cables once ran in many other places, including New York, Los Angeles, Seattle, Denver, Chicago, London, and Sydney, Australia, they were invented in San Francisco and exist nowhere else in the world today. Here and there you can find funicular cars, but their operation is different from that of San Francisco's Cables. That The City's Cables are unique befits their status as the world's first and oldest motorized urban mass transit system.

The Cables are living monuments of, not to, San Francisco's history. Like The City itself, they are romantic and sweet and comic and exciting, full of mystery and assorted, unexpected sidetracks. Because neither the Cables nor San Francisco can be explained adequately in terms of modern life alone, this book is also a guide to the past, a tour through some of the history with some of the personalities that made San Francisco what it is today.

It is the purpose of this book to enable you to enjoy both the Cables and The City as far as your time and wishes will allow. There is no single way to see San Francisco, any more than there is a single way to look at an artistic masterpiece or a rare gem. Yet, since a book must start somewhere and end somewhere, having been somewhere else meanwhile, I have divided those parts of The City served by the Cables into several discrete areas. Each may be seen as a mini-tour in itself, and you may wish to follow the progression as I've outlined it in these pages. If so, you will find I've rearranged The City a bit, specifically in order to enable you to ride the

Cable Car routes in their entirety without missing any of the most important parts of town they reach. Thus, I have included Maiden Lane with your Powell-Mason line ride, even though it is properly an adjunct of Union Square, which I have called part of your Powell-Hyde line ride. Also, I have taken you to Chinatown on the Powell-Hyde line, even though it is commonly reached via the California line. But I have also provided maps throughout this book, so that if you would prefer to see Maiden Lane as part of Union Square, or to visit Chinatown by way of the California line, you can do so with no difficulty. Feel free to pick and choose, break the guide down into its component parts, rearrange the areas to suit your own convenience, return to your favorite places more than once. In brief, use this volume in any way that will help you to see what you want to see, and to have a good time at it.

The upcoming maps show the Cable Car lines as they are today. As you can see, they cover a relatively small portion of The City's total geography (although this was not always so, as I'll explain in a few pages). If your San Francisco plans will carry you beyond the Cables' limits, you may find other guidebooks useful in addition to this one. I've included a few of my personal favorites, as well as some of my favorite places to visit, in the Appendices beginning on p. *152* . For guided tours, see Appendix C. You can also research guides and special sightseeing tours with the aid of the Convention and Visitors Bureau, located in Hallidie Plaza at Powell and Market Streets, where we will begin our Cable Car tour in jι a few pages.

If you're determined and in a hurry, you *can* cover the entire Cable Car tour in a single day. However, I suggest it will be worth several days, or even several visits to The City, to do so in a satisfying manner. The modern City, like its history, is rich and varied; it is as difficult to grasp it all at once as it is to enjoy yourself on the run.

At the end of each chapter concerning a specific area, you will find a short list of my suggestions for things you might enjoy doing or seeing, and restaurants in which you might like to dine. Please understand, I do not intend my lists to

Powell & Market Streets, c. 1890, showing the legendary Baldwin Hotel.

be exclusive or exhaustive; particularly with regard to restaurants (which dominate my listings because they must be
experienced to be appreciated, whereas much else on this
tour can be examined in the course of a walk or ride). With

regard to stores and sights of other sorts as well, it is impossible to include even the names of every place of value in a book as brief as this. I have simply singled out some personal favorites as a way of guiding you in a general way, trying to avoid places too new for their quality to be established, or places whose hold on life is sufficiently precarious to suggest they may have closed before you can get to them. In this regard, two things: In the past decade, San Francisco has been undergoing its largest new construction and rede-velopment spree since the Earthquake. It seems that a new highrise goes up, and an old block comes down, every few weeks. Consequently, many stores and restaurants have had to change their addresses too frequently for any such listing to be absolutely reliable. Therefore, I suggest you double-check current locations for those places you wish to visit, either with local acquaintances, or by calling ahead. Also, for the true gastronome, the best available guide to The City's epicurean delights is Paul Wallach's *Guide to the Restaurants of Northern California.* For bar hoppers, *Great and Notorious Saloons of San Francisco,* by Jane Chamberlin and Hank Arm-strong is a good introduction.

For the restaurants I indicate two sorts of rating marks: asterisks (***) and dollar signs ($$$). The dollar signs sig-nify the relative cost of a meal, *per person.* One dollar sign ($) means inexpensive—$10 or less; two dollar signs ($$) mean moderately priced—$10-$25; three dollar signs ($$$) mean expensive— $25 or more. Similarly, the asterisks tell you what I think of an establishment's food. No asterisk means ordinary but decent fare; one asterisk (*) means I think the place offers good food; two asterisks (**) mean I think the food is noteworthy; and three asterisks (***) signify an extraordinary dining experience. Note: in a few cases "ex-traordinary" must be taken in context. A three-asterisk ice cream parlor is not to be compared with a three-asterisk French establishment.

Please note also that my suggestions are made without the present knowledge of the various businesses' proprietors. No one paid for a listing in this book, and no payment of any kind was solicited. I encourage you to explore each area I discuss on your own, and to discover your own favorite shops, museums, restaurants, and special places you will always hold dear in your memory. Despite the hills, San Francisco is a remarkable walker's town, and many of its most lovely charms disclose themselves only to the slow procession on foot.

You will also find that many of the major hotels offer concierge services. The concierge will be able to answer your specific questions about how and where to obtain theatre tickets, make dinner reservations if possible (many San Francisco restaurants do not take reservations or credit cards), and mediate in countless other ways to make your visit to San Francisco both pleasant and memorable.

Finally, if you are an old friend of The City's, welcome back to your home away from home. If you're visiting for the first time, welcome to a unique world of wonderful experiences. I hope you'll allow the range and depth of San Francisco's background to delight and instruct you about its present features. For truly, how can you call someone a good friend unless you know at least a little something about her past?

In closing, a few suggestions:

San Francisco is not the California of travel posters—the average year-round daytime temperature is 63° F. Between November and April is the rainy season; during the summer months it is often foggy; autumn is sunny. So, it is wise to always carry a warm sweater or jacket when out and about, and an umbrella during the winter months.

Casual clothes and comfortable walking shoes will serve you best. However, dress clothes will be required in exclusive establishments or for formal occasions.

Tipping for service is the custom in San Francisco (15% of the bill is normal), as this is how cabbies, waiters, waitresses, tourguides, etc. earn their livings. However, tip according to the quality of the service.

Common sense and a smile will go a long way to making your visit safer and more enjoyable.

Be careful where you park your car—tow-away zones and other restricted parking areas on streets are strictly enforced.

San Franciscans are very proud of their city and they enjoy sharing it with others. Being respectful of this pride in your enjoyment of San Francisco will make for a worthwhile and fun experience all around.

DEDICATION

For Kathy & Crystal . . .

to Mrs. Hans Klussmann, and to all those with whom I worked on the Cable Cars.

−GTY

In San Francisco, the past is always present and the present always quite madly wonderful.

Herb Caen
San Francisco Chronicle

ACKNOWLEDGEMENTS

For all their good and kind assistance, I would like to thank the helpful staff members of: the California Historical Society, the Bancroft Library, University of California at Berkeley; the San Francisco Convention and Visitors Bureau; the San Francisco Cable Car Museum; the Wells Fargo History Museum; the Cable Car Rehabilitation Project Office at MUNI; the San Francisco History Room of the San Francisco Public Library. To the following, without whom this book, for whatever it may achieve, would not have been possible: Bill Henkin, a dearly patient and understanding comrade whose skilled editorship made my laborious manuscript a viable book; Dave Williams, whose legwork stood in for me when I was unable; Bill Yenne, whose creative design work has made this book artistic, and for introducing me to Bill Henkin; Bill Merryman, Randy Fingland, and Sheridan McCarthy of Wingbow Press/Bookpeople, for all their help and faith; Modesto Giordano, a true friend whose aid and knowledge have helped me greatly; Jim Hutchins, for his friendship and photographic skill; and to all those friends, too numerous to list here, who have each in their own special way helped make this contribution possible.

————— *George T. Young*
San Francisco
January 1st, 1984

San Francisco
by Cable Car

THE PHOENIX OF CHRYSOPYLAE:
A Brief Introduction to San Francisco's Lore

No other city or place has so captured the spirit of the goddess Columbia as this hoyden, sophisticated, elegantly brash lady named for the Italian saint who believed in love. She is the archetype of the West—and yet, for all her alluring beauty, her charm, her culture, and her history, she often seems but a paradox wrapped in an enigma

to those from outside her borders. As Oscar Wilde wryly observed, "It's an odd thing, but anyone who disappears is said to be seen in San Francisco. It must be a delightful city and possess all the attractions of the next world."

Well, it's true. San Francisco exudes a quaint and magical personality that demands satire, superlatives, metaphor, hyperbole, cliche, and even chauvinism to describe. And all are justified! But what is this personality, and how did it come to be "Baghdad-by-the-Bay?"

San Francisco was legendary even before its beginning. As with Rome and a few other centers of human culture, myth preceded fact so that San Francisco created itself from a chimerical vision of a hoped-for reality, and, incorporating

Typical Cable Car scene in the 1880's showing Car with "Dummy" or trailer. The towing of "Dummies" was discontinued early in the 20th century, the increase in auto traffic making them less safe.

every vice and virtue of the human condition, presented itself as a *fait accompli* to a world it would forever change.

The legendary explanation of California's name: About the time Columbus reached the Americas, and long before any European was knowledgeable of their Pacific coasts, Garcia O. Montalvo, an obscure writer in Spain, published a fascinating romance titled *Las Sergas de Esplandian (The Deeds of Esplandian, the Son of Amadis of Gaul)*. In his charming adventure tale the author tells of a magical island supposed to exist on the west side of the "New World." The island is described as being full of many wonders, possessed of vast, fertile lands and a climate of eternal springtime—in short, a terrestrial paradise. Even more enticing, this island is said to possess a supply of gold richer than any other on Earth, and to be populated by a race of voluptuous black Amazons ruled by a queen who commands her empire from a fabulous city by the sea. The queen is no ordinary mortal, naturally, but a goddess. Her name is *Calafia,* and after her the island is called *California*.

The first European explorations of America, after Columbus's, were led by the Spanish, and the conquest of Mexico by Cortez in 1519 brought a new, potent meaning to the legends they established of the American West. The fallen Aztecs' gold impressed the conquering Spanish more than the high state of their culture, it so fired their lust for greater riches that no tale concerning this vast new world was considered unreasonable. Therefore, Cortez and others sent out expeditions by land and by sea to search for the still more amazing places described to them in both legends and reports. Cortez himself was perhaps familiar with the myth of Calafia, but he was responsible for discovering and naming the real California, both Alta and Baja. Ironically, the early maps of the area showed California to be an island situated to the north and west of Mexico (see map, p. 12-13). No doubt Cortez and other explorers and grandees were disappointed when they failed to find Calafia's golden empire. What they could not know, of course, was that the riches and dreams of legend did exist in fact—only not in the form these eager seekers imagined. Rather, they existed in a future whose reality would have seemed far more fantastic to the explorers than an island full of exotic, dangerous women clad in gold armor.

While the Spanish were paramount in exploring and laying claim to western America, they were by no means the only Europeans who sought the new land's riches. Foremost among the others was England's Sir Francis Drake, who followed the Spaniard Cabrillo's pioneering voyage of 1542, and, at least, sailed past the Golden Gate in 1579. Whether or not Drake actually sailed into San Francisco Bay is an open question, but it is believed that he landed a few miles north of the Gate and claimed the land he named New Albion for England. Drake did not return to California, however, and it was left for the Spanish to establish the first Occidental settlements here.

Despite numerous explorations, California's interior, as well as much of its coast, remained a mystery. While Spain's claims to the land were not much contested, it was some 200 years before the Spanish did anything meaningful to develop their prize. Perhaps the delay is not surprising, considering the difficulties and hazards of travel and the riotous European political climate of that age. In any event, neither the Spanish nor any other Europeans made a serious attempt to settle California until the late 1700s. The principal colonizing expeditions were led by Captain Gaspar de Portola and the now-legendary Franciscan priest, Father Junipero Serra, who founded the historic chain of missions that runs from San Diego north to San Francisco.

In 1775, the first known navigation of San Francisco Bay was undertaken by Lieutenant Juan Manuel de Ayala. This navigation followed by six years Portola's accidental discovery of the Bay. Portola's overland party had reached Monterey, the Spanish California capital, but its Bay was not the reported huge, sheltered harbor they were seeking, so they pressed on. On November 2, while hunting deer, some of Portola's men, including Father Serra, climbed the headlands at what is now the Palo Alto area south of The City and saw from a distance what they took to be an inland sea or a lake; this was the "safe harbor" Amerindian reports had led them to expect.

Soon after de Ayala's expedition, the first *presidio,* or military fort, was built here; and Father Serra established the Mission San Francisco de Assisi (Mission Dolores). Both these events took place in 1776, a date whose significance is probably not lost on the reader of these pages. Indeed, it almost reads like myth itself to know that while the United States was being born on the east side of North America, the city that would make possible complete *Novus Ordo Seclorum* was being founded on the west side of the continent.

Due to neglect by the Spanish throne, the missions fell into almost immediate disrepair, and only in the early 1800s, when the Russians attempted to claim the lands north of San Francisco, did the Spanish demonstrate a brief resurgence of interest in protecting their claims by adding two new missions, one at San Rafael, and another at Sonoma. However, the Russians abandoned their efforts, and when Mexico became an independent republic in 1823, it accepted the missions as part of its domain. California continued to be benignly neglected under the new arrangement, much as it had been before. There were enormous ranches belonging to the California-Mexican landed gentry, however, and their pastoral culture is now a rich part of California's early romantic history—the legend of Zorro being a prime example. But if the new Mexican government's problems caused it to neglect its northern territories, that of the young United States was starting to pay them serious attention. As the first major caravans of wagons and carts began to move west across the plains, a little trickle of migration soon became a steady stream.

By the late 1830s, the United States government could no longer fail to attend to the prospects of the lands that lay to its west. Reports from such explorers as Lewis and Clark concerning the Northwest, the obvious strategic value of San Francisco's harbor, and the fact that both England and France had initiated political maneuvers designed to take over the area, all combined with the American concept of Manifest

Destiny to ensure that the fate of California would be, indeed, an American one. In the 1840s, when the annexation of Texas was being hotly debated in Washington, D.C., Daniel Webster summed up the attitudes of many government officials, saying, "You know my opinion to have been, and it is now, that the port of San Francisco would be twenty times as valuable to us as all Texas."

Between 1842 and 1850 profound changes swept California, and San Francisco in particular, in a frenzy of hectic confusion that has become one of the great sagas of all human history. Increasing numbers of settlers poured into the territory, and relations between Mexico and the United States deteriorated. Popular support for an American California provided the final rationale for the United States to seize the land, supposedly as a means of preventing European powers from taking it first. A cavalier and sometimes ruthless United States Army officer named John Charles Fremont, with Kit Carson as his guide, made his first expedition into Calafia's realm, and began the formal process of securing California for his government.

It should be noted that it was Colonel Fremont who formally named the entrance to San Francisco's harbor. An engineer as well as a soldier, Fremont was the first person commissioned by the U.S. Government to survey San Francisco Bay. In his records he referred to the opening to the Pacific Ocean as *Chrysopylae*. The word is Latin, but derives from the ancient Greek, and means "gate of gold," or "city with a gate of gold," or "city of the golden gate." It shall be left to the poets to speculate whether Fremont's choice of a name, preceding the discovery of gold in the nearby hills, should be thought prophetic. I do note, however, without implying a serious connection between them, that the fabulous capital city of the mythical Atlantis—like San Francisco, destroyed by earthquake—also bore the name City of the Golden Gate.

Without belaboring the swift changes that followed, the historical scenario went more or less like this: In May, 1846, after fighting several small skirmishes, the United States declared war on Mexico. The Mexican headquarters at Sonoma was swiftly taken, followed soon thereafter by the Mexican California capital at Monterey. At Sonoma, American forces surprised the great Mexican General Guadalupe Vallejo, and he surrendered without bloodshed. Then, wholly independent of any existing government's intentions, local settlers took matters into their own hands and established the short-lived Bear Flag Republic, with its capital at Sonoma. This made California a "separate country" for a few weeks. (The Golden Bear flag adopted by these revolutionaries was later chosen to be the official flag of the State of California.)

Soon thereafter, Captain John B. Montgomery, commanding the United States warship *Portsmouth,* entered San Francisco Bay and landed his troops where Portsmouth Square stands today, off Kearny Street, next to Chinatown. He took the village, then known as Yerba Buena, without serious incident. Within weeks, all of California was a formally secured United States possession.

Hard on the heels of these military exploits, of course, came the greatest event of them all: the discovery of gold in 1848. This single most important event in the history of the American West greatly accelerated the process of California's achieving statehood, which it did in September, 1850.

Gold. Early in the American immigration to California, an enterprising Swiss entrepreneur and soldier of fortune, Captain John Sutter, created a private little empire for himself centered around a fort on the Sacramento River northeast of San Francisco, called New Helvetia. This town would later become the site of the state capital, Sacramento. Sutter was sympathetic to the arriving American and European settlers and their cause, and built a lucrative business supplying them with tools and food. In fact, his business thrived so well that he found it necessary to expand. And so, in the fall of 1847, about one year after the American flag was first raised over San Francisco, Sutter employed a recently-arrived contractor, John Marshall, to build a small lumber mill on the American River, about 50 miles northeast of Sutter's fort. In January, 1848, while inspecting the workings around the mill's foundation, Marshall's attention was drawn to something glittering, glinting, and shining in the water. It was yellow. It was metal. It was not pyrite.

Although Marshall's discovery of gold initiated a period of history whose global consequences included the greatest purposeful migration of humanity since the Crusades, the actual event possessed surprisingly little of the dramatic. When Marshall and Sutter discussed the find, they apparently decided it would not amount to much, and that it would be prudent to keep the matter secret, at least until the season's work had been completed and some sort of preparations could be made for dealing with the find. But neither Marshall's practical sense nor Sutter's business wisdom could hide such news for long. Someone, perhaps in all innocence, spilled the beans.

One of Sutter's friends was Sam Brannan, a leading citizen of the village that was San Francisco and the vociferous publisher of the *California Star,* one of the first major newspapers in the early West. Somehow, Brannan learned of the discovery. He was far more taken with the possibilities he saw embodied in the gold than he was with any problems, real or imagined, that might accrue to Sutter once the news got out. Brannan is reported to have dashed down the primitive, muddy roadway that was then Montgomery Street, waving a bottle of gold dust over his head and bellowing at the top of his lungs, "Gold! Gold!!! GOLD from the American River!" And suddenly, according to legend, only seven men were left in town.

Whether the story of Brannan and his bottle is true or fanciful, gold fever exploded into real life with an element of romance so unique and transforming in its character that few events in the pixilated affairs of mankind can compare with it. The prospects of grand adventure, new life in a utopian land, dreams that might be realized, and exploits that might be pursued—and above all the very real possibility of fabulous, limitless wealth—caused a madcap dash to San Francisco and the gold fields of California that can only be described as a fantastic and unprecedented phenomenon. No one, in his very wildest imaginings, would have predicted the enormity of riches to which Sutter's find would lead. In the single year of 1852, for example, the area's gold production amounted to more than $81 million. Translated into today's coin the amount would exceed many billions in buying power. In that era without taxes, with ludicrously cheap labor,* apparently boundless, inexpensive resources, and a political policy of *laissez-faire* everything, the effect of so vast a sum was nothing less than staggering to the small population that fell heir to it. This was the amount produced in a single year, remember. Sums equal to and larger than that continued to flow into San Francisco regularly for more than an entire generation.

In 1847 Rincon de las Salinas had been able to write of San Francisco, "We find her with a population of less than 400, with no commerce, no wealth, no power, and without a name, save as a small trading post and mission station." But as news of gold reached New York, London, and other world centers, the primitive little hamlet by the sea was torn apart and transformed almost overnight into a city and world mecca. In the fabled year of 1849, before the first great waves of invaders stormed into town, the nameless trading post was the talk of the civilized world.

Soon after news of the gold got out, the trading post's population swelled to more than 5000;† within ten years some 80,000 people from every corner of the earth were living here, and the rivers of humanity that kept flowing in seemed endless. The hordes that passed through San Francisco on their ways to the gold fields amounted to several hundred thousand more. By 1900, San Francisco and the Bay Area had become a world metropolis whose population exceeded a half-million. It was the eighth largest city in the United States, second only to New York in the value of its

---

* In many respects, labor began to be very well paid early in The City's history. However, many people, such as the immigrant Chinese, were shamelessly exploited.

† Statistics from this era vary from one source to another. My figures are round number estimates derived by averaging those available from historical sources.

foreign and domestic trade and as a port and cultural center. The armies of forty-niners, or Argonauts (so-called after the men who sailed with Jason on the Argo in search of the mythical golden fleece), represented every nation, class, race, and type of human being, and they transformed California into a very real El Dorado. The mythical golden empire of Calafia became an indisputable fact of life.

One can well imagine the kind of glorious excess that sudden wealth of this magnitude unleashed upon a totally unprepared little village that had almost no established law or government. Indeed, every vice and all the Seven Deadly Sins ran riot for a time, both in the streets of San Francisco and in the gold fields. From this condition of debauchery arose the infamous Barbary Coast (see p. *120*), and some measure of San Francisco's extravagant style and the Babylonian nature of her pleasure-seeking.

San Francisco's early lawlessness caused the fledgling city to be levelled by fire six times in three years. Because of this, in 1852 the first city officials—once more inspired by myth—chose for the City Seal and the official symbol of San Francisco, the Phoenix: the fabulous bird of ancient Egypt that repeatedly arose from its own ashes, symbolizing peerless beauty, resurrection, and, to some, a copiously liberal, limitlessly rich immortality. Considering the alacrity, strength, and enthusiasm with which San Francisco has repeatedly sprung from her own ashes, and the success with which she revived from the devastation wrought by the Great Earthquake and Fire of 1906 (still the worst disaster to befall any American city), the Phoenix remains a strikingly fit emblem.

Fate was cruel to Sutter and Marshall. They lost everything, save their places in history as the first to uncover Calafia's trove. But the city built by their discovery matured quickly, with an optimism, openness, and exuberance unique in the world, and it rapidly became one of the great cultural and commercial centers on earth. Its wealth, reputation, and beauty, its civility, spirit, and style, became, in the space of little more than a generation, a benchmark for the

Until the late 18th century California was thought to be an island, from the legend of Calafia. This 1718 map is typical of early maps showing the "Island of California."

other great cities of the globe. "The City," as it came to be called by its inhabitants, was soon known everywhere as the Queen City of the West, offering "a little of Rome, a little of Paris, a little of Peking." Because of its special Bohemian atmosphere of tolerance and amusement, it became a creative haven for new ideas and the avant-garde in art, politics, and

social intercourse. In the process, it took on the status of a quasi-city-state.

So much for the general background about this fabled place. More needs to be said, of course, about the particulars; and it shall be said, as we go along. For a start, if you'll just turn the page, I'd like to introduce you to what former Cable Car gripman John Tobiasson refers to as "the most beloved, valuable, peculiar, and only usefully functional anachronism in America."

THE LAST MAGIC CARPET:
A Brief History of the Cable Cars

"They take no count of rise or fall," Rudyard Kipling wrote of The City's unofficial symbol. "They turn corners almost at right angles, cross other lines and for aught I know may turn up the sides of houses . . . If it pleases Providence to make a car run up and down a slit in the ground, why shall I ask the reason for the miracle?"

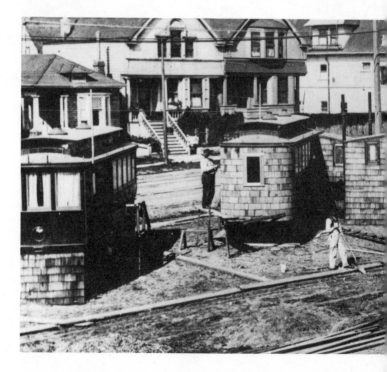

A miracle indeed. But the real miracle is not so much that such a wonderfully comic mode of transportation actually works—which is a phenomenon in itself—but rather that it is *still* working after more than a century, to the joy and delight of millions of people each year. They are utterly unique—a transcendental transport system sublime.

On August 2, 1873, an English-born engineer and businessman, Andrew Hallidie, launched the world's first Cable Car down Clay Street from the top of Nob Hill at Jones Street. This event not only inaugurated the first fleet of what was to become San Francisco's most beloved emblem; it also marked the start of mechanized public transportation on the streets of any city. As soon as "Hallidie's Folly," as the grand contraption was called, proved itself to be both practical and

A rare photo showing Cable Cars converted into emergency housing after the 1906 Earthquake.

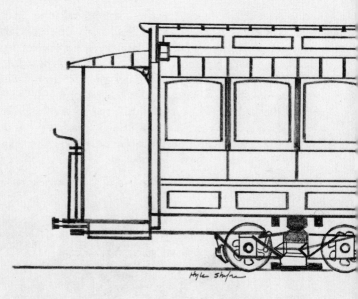

A side view schematic of a Powell-type Car showing workings of brakes, grip, trucks, and other major mechanical features.

profitable, London, New York, Denver, Los Angeles, and other urban centers began installing cable lines of their own. Cable technology is cumbersome, however, and operating costs fairly high; so, when the more advanced electric trolleys (streetcars or trams) became feasible in the late 1880s, they replaced cable traction rail cars—the technical description for streetcars pulled by underground cables—almost everywhere.

But not in San Francisco. Electric trolleys could not climb this City's notorious hills, and they were not much used here as Cable Car replacements even on the flatter streets until

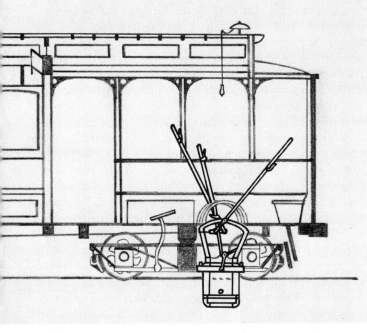

after the Earthquake. Until that time, Cable Cars travelled as many as 112 miles of track under the auspices of about a dozen companies reaching almost all parts of San Francisco's neighborhoods. Eventually, diesel and electric trolley buses—which *could* climb the hills—picked off most of the old Cable Car lines until, by the 1940s, the only Cable lines remaining were essentially those still in use today, now all operated by the Municipal Railway System of San Francisco (MUNI), which also has jurisdiction over the local buses and streetcars.

In the 1940s, with the Cable Car a severely endangered species, even these last three lines stood poised on the brink of extinction. "Progressives" in The City's government wanted more modern buses, and pressed their desires with increasing ferocity, until Mrs. Hans Klussmann arrived on the scene, fighting for the Cables' lives. The bitter battle that resulted between Mrs. Klussmann and the Cables' supporters, on one side, and the "bus people" at City Hall on the other, mobilized tens of thousands of San Franciscans sympathetic to the preservationists, and elicited cries of support from around the world. Soon, an indignant Mayor Lapham and his cronies, damned by the public, conceded defeat; and the "crazy little cars" were cheered to their victory with a demonstration worthy of The City's freespirited tradition. The ad hoc organization Mrs. Klussmann founded succeeded in having the Cables declared a National Landmark of the Federal Government, and in having a San Francisco City Charter amendment passed protecting them as well.

But even Mrs. Klussmann's noble efforts were not a guarantee for the Cables' preservation. Age and bureaucratic snafus had taken their toll, and following the Cars' centennial celebration in 1973 the system began to deteriorate rapidly. By 1979, the antique machinery was literally falling apart, and was becoming a safety hazard. At that time the system was shut down for six months for emergency repairs. It was all too apparent that the entire system would have to be rebuilt if its wheels were going to keep on turning.

A new Committee to Save the Cable Cars was formed, and a Save the Cable Cars campaign began, led by prominent political leaders and businessmen and women, with a now elderly Mrs. Klussmann serving as chairperson emeritus. It was estimated that rehabilitation would cost in excess of $58 million. The Federal government agreed to provide $44 million, and the State of California $3 million. The people and businesses of San Francisco were responsible for about $10 million.

They rallied behind the cause. With large corporate contributions from such companies as Chevron USA, Kaiser Aluminum, Natomas, American Airlines, Mitsubishi, Levi Strauss, most of The City's major hotels and department stores, as well as tens of thousands of individuals, money was raised from all sorts of civic and public functions from rock concerts to marathon races. As you can see, it all worked. On

September 21, 1982, the 109-year-old system rattled and clanged to a halt amid an official City day of celebration that attracted hundreds of thousands of people and lasted until the wee hours of the morning. Work to rebuild the system began the next day, and in June and July, 1984, like another phoenix, the new Cable Car system officially leapt to life again with another grand celebration heard 'round the world. The Official Re-opening Celebration is set for June 21, 1984.

This new system looks and works virtually like the old one. Only the adept observer will be able to notice the changes. As it is a National Landmark, no major alterations were permitted. However, machinery under the street and in the Powerhouse has been rebuilt and updated, new track has been laid, and so on. Even though what you ride on today is "new," it is still "old," and essentially the same as what your great-great-grandfather would have ridden on had he visited San Francisco. The cars themselves are the originals and are being restored.

The quaint custom of the Conductor pulling the fare box lever to register fares may or may not have become lamented memory by the time you read this. Today, numbered tickets are issued from machines, as well as from the Conductors on the Cars themselves. The ticket machine locations are planned:

    *at each Cable Car terminal
    *at the intersection of Powell and Post
    *at the intersection of Powell and California
    *at the Cable Car Barn

Several types of fare tickets will be available, as well as a day excursion ticket good for "all day." The current basic one-way fare is $1.00 for adults. There are discounts of various sorts for senior citizens and children, and transfers from MUNI bus and streetcar lines. The attendant at each terminal, the Conductor and Gripman on each Cable Car, and the people who work at the Cable Car Barn will be able to provide you with up-to-date or more specific information should you require it.

However, so brief a history for so unique an aspect of Americana as the Cables cannot begin to do justice to the full

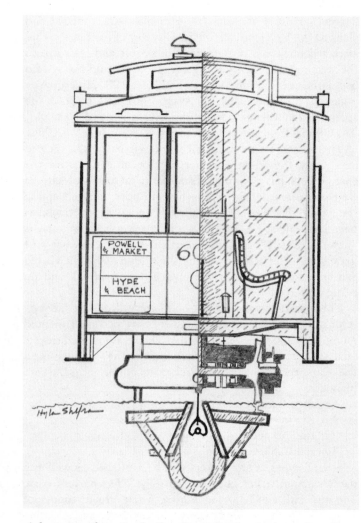

A front view schematic of a Powell-type Car showing how grip works & other significant features.

story. Indeed, just the story of the rebuilding would require a book. It would be a fairly safe bet that every famous, important, and/or notorious person who has visited San Francisco in the past hundred-plus years has ridden on one or another of these Cars. Kings and princesses, presidents and statesmen, movie stars and celebrities of every description, gangsters and bums, hookers and pimps, captains of business and industry, beatniks and hippies, business people going to and from work, tourists and locals out for a good time—the Cable Car has been the Big Heart that has befriended them all equally. The Cables have carried the United States mail and a little boy's Shetland pony. They provided emergency housing after The City's 1906 disaster. They have been the stage for weddings, political campaigns, and parties of all sorts, official and unofficial. They have been festooned with floral displays and floats for festive occasions. You name it, and it probably happened on a Cable Car—including the incident that prompted one buxom blonde to sue The City— and win $50,000!—alleging that falling off a Cable Car caused her to become a nymphomaniac.

*   *   *

"Looks like some kind of Rube Goldberg contraption," a traveler smiled to me one day.

"Right," I said, "but you have it the wrong way around. You see, Rube Goldberg was from San Francisco. . . ."

As you might expect from so ancient a mechanical marvel, the Cable Cars are rather primitive and straightforward in their simple engineering, albeit confusingly complicated in the mechanics of their operation. Like most mysteries, however, the operation of the Cables is simpler than it first appears. It is rather like an elevator or lift laid on its side on wheels running on a track. The motive power for the Cable Cars is a continuous loop of heavy steel cable called the "rope," which runs along under the street, below a slot opening between the rails, at a steady nine miles per hour. All the miles of rope come from and return to the Power-house, today pulled around and around by four 500 hp electric motors that drive all three remaining cable contrivances through four cables, one motor for each cable. The use of four motors is new; prior to the restoration two 750 hp motors were used, with only one operating at a time to drive all the cables. In the early days it was a steam engine that powered the rope, and since there were many more Cable lines than there are today, there were also several other

Powerhouses scattered about The City. The present Power-house is located at the Cable Car Barn, which also incorporates the Cable Car Museum and Powerhouse Gift Shop. This complex is open daily, and is an unusual must-see on your San Francisco agenda. It is best reached on the Powell-Mason line or the Powell-Hyde line, on your way to or from the Fisherman's Wharf Area (see p. 67).

The Cars themselves move along the rope by way of a device known as the "grip." The grip is the central of the large levers you can see on the Car in front of the driver. It is the one he pulls when he wants the Car to move forward or uphill. The grip works rather like a huge pair of pliers: it fits down through the Car and into the slot between the rails, closing around the cable or rope, "gripping" it to achieve forward motion. Because of this device, the person who drives the Cable Car is properly called a Cable Car Gripman. His co-worker, who moves about the Car collecting fares and who goes to the rear of the Car to operate the rear brake, is called the Conductor.

The large lever to the right of the grip as you face in your direction of travel is the main brake, or track brake, so named because it stops the Car by pushing blocks of wood down onto the track. The friction that results from the operation of the track brake sometimes causes an odor of burning wood; this is no cause for alarm. In spite of what a novice to the Cable system may imagine, looking at the hills the Cables climb, these brakes have proven themselves remarkably effective and safe. Besides, there are some backup measures. On the single-ended Powell Street Cars, there is a brake lever at the rear of each Car, which operates a set of drum wheel brakes; the conductor activates this backup when the Car is descending hills. In addition, there is a foot brake which is an additional pedal-operated wheel brake you may see the Grip-man standing on from time to time, which likewise presses steel shoes against the wheels of the Car, working much as do the drum brakes of an automobile. On the double-ended California Cars, the Conductor works both track and wheel brakes in conjunction with the Gripman, when descending hills. In the rare and unlikely event that all else fails, the red lever to the left and forward of the grip is the "slot brake," or emergency brake, which will drive a steel wedge into the cable slot with extreme force, stopping the car quite suddenly. In fact, when a Gripman has to use the emergency brake, the steel wedge often secures itself into the slot so well that a welding torch is required to free the Car afterwards. And for rainy days, when the tracks grow slick, the Gripman can push a foot-operated lever to release jets of sand onto the tracks, enhancing traction. Feel better?

The happy, world-famous bell on the roof of each Car is rung by a cord hanging in front of the Gripman, and by tradition it has become a percussion instrument as well as a warning signal. Many of the Gripmen are highly accomplished bell-ringers, and punctuate the lumbering din of the streets with their unique musical offerings. In fact, there is an annual Cable Car bell-ringing contest held in the summer or autumn as part of The City's civic functions, in which the best of the bell-ringers compete for prizes and honor.

The small bells, up on the ceiling at each end of every Car, are operated by the cord which runs the length of the Car, also up near the ceiling. These bells are used for intra-Car communication between the Gripman and the Conductor in a sort of code. The principal signals are: one bell = stop; two bells = go. If you hear a rapid staccato on the small bells it probably means one Cable Car crew is saying hello to another or that a pretty woman is walking by. For obvious reasons, do not pull this bell cord; tell the Conductor or Gripman where you want to get off.

(Note: As already mentioned, but important enough to emphasize again, some of the preceding data on how the Cables function, fares, etc., will likely be altered slightly by the time you read this—the lead time necessary to produce this book being enough ahead of MUNI's final decision-making to preclude fully accurate information being possible for this edition. For up-to-the-minute information ask your Gripman or Conductor, MUNI personnel at terminals, or the fine staff at the Cable Car Museum. You can also phone MUNI directly at 673-MUNI, or ask your host at your hotel.)

BALLAD OF THE
HYDE STREET GRIP

by
GELETT BURGESS

Oh, the rain is slanting sharply, and the Norther's blowing cold,
When the cable strands are loosened she is nasty hard to hold;
There's little time for sitting down and little time for gab,
For the bumper guards the crossing, and you'd best be keeping tab!
Two-and-twenty "let-go's" every double trip—
It takes a bit of doing on the Hyde Street Grip!'

Throw her off at Powell street, let her go at Post,
Watch her well at Geary and at Sutter, when you coast,
Easy at the Power House, have a care at Clay,
Sacramento, Washington, Jackson, all the way!
Drop the rope at Union, never make a slip—
The lever keeps you busy on the Hyde Street Grip!

Foot-brake, wheel-brake, slot-brake and gong,
You've got to keep 'em working, or you'll be going wrong!

Rush her on the crossing, catch her on the rise,
Easy round the corners, when the dust is in your eyes!
And the bell will always stop you, if you hit her up a clip—
You are apt to earn your wages, on the Hyde Street Grip!

North Beach to the Tenderloin, over Russian Hill,
The grades are something giddy and the curves are fit to kill!
All the way to Market Street, climbing up the slope,
Down upon the other side, hanging to the rope;
But the sight of San Francisco as you take the lurching dip!
There is plenty of excitement on the Hyde Street Grip!

Oh, the lights are in the Mission and the ships are in the Bay;
And Tamalpais is looming from the Gate across the way;
The Presidio trees are waving and the hills are growing brown!
And the driving fog is harried from the Ocean to the town!
How the pulleys slap and rattle! How the cables hum and whip!
Oh, they sing a gallant chorus on the Hyde Street Grip!

When the Orpheum is closing and the crowd is on the way,
The conductor's punch is ringing and the dummy's light and gay;
But the wait upon the table by the Beach is dark and still—
Just the swashing of the surges on the shore below the mill;
And the flash of Angel Island breaks across the channel rip,
And the hush of midnight falls upon the Hyde Street Grip!

THE POWELL-HYDE LINE
Powell and Market

Unless you have arrived very early in the morning or very late at night, you will find waiting in line at this little depot, which was recently reconstructed around the new turntable, an unavoidable nuisance. But, as with most good things in life, the wait is worthwhile. It is something of an enforced pause in your day's occupation that can be both informative and entertaining.

If knowledge is your bent, you might wish to learn that the huge Emporium department store right across Market Street from where you are standing was the first true department store on the Pacific coast. When it opened its doors in 1896, it was among the largest stores of any kind anywhere in the world. Or you might enjoy knowing about the Flood Building, the majestic, gray stone structure just beside the turntable, whose ground floor houses the world's busiest Woolworth's. Erected by railroad magnate James Flood at the turn of the century, and restored after it suffered major damage in the 1906 conflagration, part of this building's fascination lies in what it replaced; for on this site once stood

Union Square looking west from Stockton St., April 1st, 1905. Note the Hotel St. Francis & the Admiral Dewey Monument.

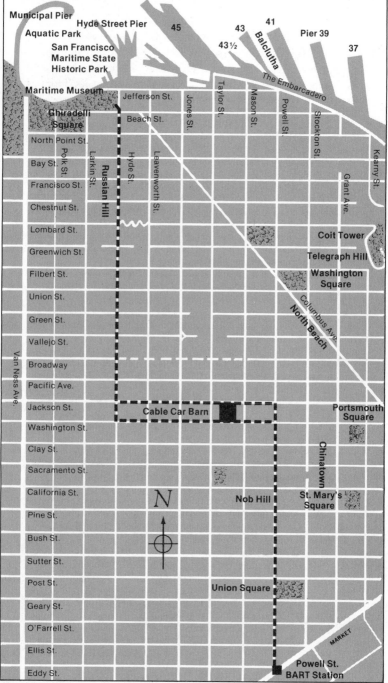

the legendary Baldwin Theatre and Hotel, owned by Elias
Jackson "Lucky" Baldwin, and destroyed by fire in the late
1890s.

Lucky Baldwin, who arrived in The City during the Gold
Rush, embodied the cunning, con-artist, wheeling-and-
dealing approach to business on which entrepreneurs prided
themselves in the heyday of *laissez-faire* capitalism. He was
not a bad fellow, by all reports; but the shrewd dealings for
which he and his kind were admired, and which were regarded as smart over a century ago, today would be considered a bit unethical. Without extending myself too far into
the well-known abuses and the occasionally humorous tactics
tycoons such as Baldwin developed, I might observe that the
prevailing public attitude in his day was a sort of *caveat emptor
in extremis*. Roughly translated, it meant, "If you're dumb
enough to get screwed, then you deserve to be."

Thus, Baldwin got rich the way most millionaires got rich
in San Francisco in those days—not by mining silver or gold,
but by exploiting real estate, stocks, commodities, construction investments, and trade.

After Baldwin made his first fortune—he made and lost
several during his lifetime—he did what *nouveau riche* gentlemen were supposed to do: he travelled. When he returned
from India and the Orient, he brought with him a team of
Japanese wrestlers and jugglers, believed to have been the
first Oriental acrobats ever to cross the Pacific. The team was
a sensation in San Francisco, so Baldwin took the members
on a tour of the United States—making another fortune—
before selling the act to an Englishman named W.S. Gilbert.
Gilbert took them to London, where they inspired him and
his partner, Sir Arthur Sullivan, to write *The Mikado*.

This Oriental vaudeville act inspired Baldwin, too. The
grand theatre and hotel he built upon his next return to San
Francisco was a splendor of Victorian gingerbread valued at
three million turn-of-the-century dollars. At its opening,
Iago, in Shakespeare's *Othello*, was played by Eugene
O'Neill's father.

Sometimes, Baldwin was beneficent as well as shrewd.
One San Francisco newsboy he befriended off the streets rose

to become a star actor and manager of Baldwin's theatre, just as Lucky had promised. Then the boy, whose name was David Belasco, went on to manage the great old Madison Square Theatre in New York, and became producer-writer of such famous hits as *The Girl of the Golden West,* which Puccini later turned into an opera.

Across Powell Street from the Flood Building stands another typical turn-of-the-century building that currently houses one of the seemingly endless branches of the Bank of America. I'll speak about this bank, though not this particular branch of it, later on p. *129* . For now, note the great, sunken, open-air pit in front of it, beside the Cable Car turntable. This is Hallidie Plaza, named in honor of the Cable Car's inventor. The Plaza houses the International Tourist Center of the San Francisco Convention and Visitors Bureau, which I urge you to visit as a major resource of maps and information in all major languages. The Plaza's primary function is to serve as the entrance/exit for the Powell Street Station of the BART system, the ultra-modern electric train/subway that connects The City to Berkeley, Oakland and other suburbs. A ride on BART (Bay Area Rapid Transit) will provide a refreshing contrast between the piquancies of modern travel and those of a bygone age, which you'll experience shortly. Don't get out of line, though; you can always return to BART later on. This is also one of the entrances to the MUNI METRO, the underground streetcar system which serves only San Francisco.

By now you may also have found yourself amused by the motley menagerie of eccentrics, vagabonds, fanatics preaching hellfire salvation (or damnation), street artists, pickpockets, pimps, and assorted Admirals of the Red. These people should be regarded strictly as some of the many varieties of "street entertainment" San Francisco offers. Many, sadly, are *real* bums whose only source of income is what they can beg or steal as the opportunity presents itself. Most of them are relatively harmless, however, and there is no cause for you to be unduly alarmed. Ignore them for the most part, and if, on occasion, some high-quality musicians, mimes, or other performers offer up their arts, allow them the decent thank-you they deserve when they pass the hat.

Now, before you board your Car, there are a few simple rules you ought to know in order to get the most Cable pleasure for your riding dollar.

Basic Cable Car Regulations and Safety Rules

1. NEVER attempt to get off or on a Car while it is moving. NEVER run after a Car or in front of one. ALWAYS step off a Car in the direction of travel. WATCH for passing autos and Cable Cars.

2. ALWAYS hold on tight, even when the Car is stopped.

3. NEVER lean out or play around on a Car.

4. NEVER touch, hold or grab the cords, levers, or other apparatus on a Car.

5. DO NOT stand behind the Gripman (the driver). ALWAYS keep doorways, exits, and work areas clear at all times, and as requested by the Conductor or Gripman; don't argue, please.

6. ALWAYS cooperate with requests from Car personnel; their jobs are to ensure a safe, pleasant ride for you, and their job is not an easy one. Cable Cars can be dangerous, so please heed the Gripman and Conductor and help to reduce accidents and stress.

7. HAVE your fare, ticket, or transfer ready for the Conductor when he or she asks for it. DO NOT try to change large bills on the Car. The current basic adult fare is $1.00. Consult Cable crews or other MUNI personnel for current rates, transfer regulations, round-trip ticket information, etc. Call 673-MUNI or ask at your hotel.

8. NEVER rush, push or shove when boarding or leaving a Car; be especially considerate of elderly passengers and children. DO NOT try to force your way onto an obviously overcrowded Car. Note: Full cars will not stop to pick up passengers.

9. ALWAYS hold onto small children, and PAY ATTENTION to what is happening around you. LOOK, and be careful.

10. IF YOU ARE DRIVING while in The City, remember that Cable Cars, like pedestrians, have the right of way *at all times*. ALWAYS YIELD. NEVER get in front of a Car on a hill or block the tracks anywhere, and if you hear a Cable Car bell clanging behind you, *get out of the way*. Be extremely careful when passing a Car. DON'T SPEED PLEASE.

11. Transfers and tickets can allow you to get on and off a Car without paying another fare. Ask your Conductor or Gripman to explain how they work.

12. Oh, and NEVER call a Cable Car a trolley . . .

As you can see on the map on p. *28* , two of the three Cable Car lines—the Powell-Mason and the Powell-Hyde—run on the same set of tracks at this juncture, and they do not diverge until they pass over the top of Nob Hill. Then the Mason line turns off on Mason Street to travel down through North Beach to Fisherman's Wharf, while the Hyde line goes over Russian Hill via Hyde Street and down to Ghirardelli Square and the Cannery complex, four blocks west of the Wharf. The best way to see all the sights these two lines afford is to take the Hyde line down to Ghirardelli, take your Wharf Area stroll in an easterly direction, explore the Cannery, Wharf, and Pier 39 (all of which we shall discuss at p. *67*), and return in this direction on the Mason line. The simplest way to distinguish one line from another here, while they're on the same tracks, is to look up on the side of the Car near the roof, where a long signboard displays the name of each Car's line. However, if you're not sure, ask your Conductor or Gripman when boarding.

In a few blocks, as your Powell-Hyde Car clangs up this bustling end of Powell Street, a grassy park with tall palm trees, known as Union Square, will appear on your right, and the St. Francis Hotel on your left. The St. Francis is one of The City's grand hotels that survived the Great Earthquake and Fire to carry on the noble heritage of San Francisco's Golden Era. If you like, you can get off the Cable Car here, step into the hotel lobby and have a drink at the Compass Rose lounge while we relive some of this marvellous hostel-

Looking up Powell Street from near Union Square in the 1880's. The block-square Stanford & Hopkins mansions dominate the crest of the hill.

ry's brilliant history as one of The City's dearest and most prestigious establishments. Then I'll tell you something about Union Square itself.

Union Square

The St. Francis

The Hotel St. Francis became part of San Francisco legend in the spring of 1904, from the very beginning far exceeding the promise of its builders that it would be a "caravansary worthy of standing at the threshold of the Occident and as the representative of California hospitality." For several days at its opening, the management entertained the general public, inviting all and sundry to inspect the hotel's rooms, and establishing the St. Francis as a focal point for The City's social life. Thoughtful architectural planning, the best in service, the most elegant new materials, and a philosophy of opulence that counted neither pennies nor dollars allowed the original management to create an ideal hotel for its day—a tradition that has continued into the present. Among its charming extravagances, for instance, is the hotel's Money Laundry, in which every coin passed on to a guest is washed beforehand. The service was originally provided so that proper ladies would not soil their white gloves handling filthy lucre; today it is at least a delightful anachronism entirely fitting along the Cable Car route.

Past and present, the elegance and courtesy proffered by the St. Francis has enticed the high and mighty of every professional pursuasion. Presidents and celebrities from McKinley, Eisenhower, and Teddy Roosevelt to Paderewski, Charlie Chaplin, and the Barrymores have called the St. Francis home when they were in town. Royalty, rulers, ambassadors, and other foreign dignitaries are so often in residence that the hotel long ago established a tradition of flying the national flags of honored guests over the main entrance on Powell Street, providing Union Square shoppers and Cable Car riders with the pleasant games of identifying flags and guessing who in the world's news is staying in the suites above.

In many ways, 1904 in San Francisco would be the perfect time and place to choose if you had a time machine and could return to any of the thrilling days of yesteryear. A new century had been born, and all over the western world people were seeking and finding the high-life pleasures for which The City had become justly famous during the Victorian era just ended. San Francisco was full of optimism and enthusiasm, and was wholly unprepared for the morning of April 18, 1906.

"Until the Fire and Earthquake of 1906 put a period to its golden age and unreconstructed ways," wrote Lucius Beebe in *San Francisco's Golden Era,*

"San Francisco clung to the grand manner. It is notable that the most expensive convocation of musical talent in the entire world, including Caruso, Eames, Sembrich, Plancon, Rossi, Hertz, Alten, and Van Rooey was playing at the Opera House, and that the first casualty of the Quake at

5:13 in the morning was the magnificent crystal chandelier above the orchestra stall, reported to be the finest and most costly in the entire world. The crash of its falling was perhaps the loudest concussion, figuratively speaking, in America until the stock market debacle of 1929, for it sounded the end of a way of life."

The newness had hardly begun to wear off the St. Francis when the disaster struck. Had it not been for the ensuing fire, the St. Francis, like the Palace (see p. *102*), the Fairmont (see p. *147*), and the rest of San Francisco's Class A buildings, would have suffered little more than some unpleasant cosmetic damage. But, alas, the three-day holocaust consumed almost everything in the entire Downtown area, and the majestic new hotel was no exception. Miraculously, however, the superstructure of the St. Francis was so sound that it withstood both the quake and the blaze intact. Reconstruction began almost immediately, and a small, temporary hotel was erected in Union Square even as work on the larger edifice commenced. Spirits remained surprisingly high. Management went out of its way to provide at least some of the amenities of good living despite the rubble. Visitors were given tours of the ruins upon which restoration was being accomplished at a feverish pace (as it was on virtually everything in town). While nothing whatsoever was in order, the Merchants Association of San Francisco held its annual banquet in the old hotel's basement, "the crumbling walls, and charred and blackened timbers hidden under a mass of bunting and foliage and flowers," as Clarence E. Edwords recollected some years later in his classic book *Bohemian San Francisco*. "Here was emphasized the spirit of Bohemian San Francisco, and it was one of the most merry and enjoyable feasts ever held in The City." Quite an exalted assessment, as you shall see.

It took a little less than two years for the St. Francis to re-open its doors (and about sixty more before its new tower addition was built to accomodate a growing influx of visitors), and it did so in style. An electrically-lit phoenix rose from a model of the burning City to greet guests as they

Contemporary photo of a Powell & Hyde Car as it lumbers along a residential segment of its route.

passed under the main entryway to a baronial banquet whose centerpiece was an illuminated model of the newly-restored hotel. Waiters carried flaming ices around the long banquet tables. Guests sat and trod upon W. & J. Sloane furnishings, ate with Reed & Barton silver from Nathan-Dohrmann china, and looked at French Gobelin tapestries that cost $100,000 apiece in the coin of the day. Marble, gold leaf, and rich woods provided appropriate backgrounds for the fittings. To introduce the hotel's new Colonial Ballroom, San Francisco socialite Mrs. Henry T. Scott threw a bash that was reported to be "the most brilliant event on the Pacific Coast." A few years later, Art Hickman introduced jazz to The City's social set here.

Paramount in the success of the St. Francis was its fabled master chef Victor Hirtzler who, along with then General Manager James Woods, refused to allow San Francisco's grand manner to die without a struggle, inconveniences such as earthquakes, fires, and rebuilding notwithstanding.

Hirtzler had come to the St. Francis after serving as chef to King Don Carlos of Portugal and official taster to Czar Nicholas II of Russia. His international reputation had been built on such extravaganzas of the table that it was said he contributed to Portugal's bankruptcy and the consequent assassination of Don Carlos. What Hirtzler loved about San Francisco was that not only was his art appreciated by a large, eager, sophisticated, and generous audience; but also, he was given free rein to create whatever gastronomic delights and sumptuous feasts he wished, without concern for expense or politics. During his 19 years as master chef at the St. Francis, Hirtzler became one of The City's living wonders. Although his classic work, *The Hotel St. Francis Cookbook,* does not contain recipes for all 136 new egg dishes he created, it is nonetheless a tome of joy for any serious cook. Victor's, the award-winning restaurant at the top of the St. Francis Tower, is named after him.

Since the early days of the hotel's existence, it has been traditional for people to meet under the antique grandfather clock in the main lobby. If you plan to join up with some local friends today, this might be a good place to do so.

Union Square

Back outside now, through the hotel's Powell Street doors, you are facing Union Square across the Cable Car tracks. This area has been known as "Downtown" to San Franciscans for a century. Its focus is the collection of famous shops and department stores surrounding the open-air plaza and extending in all directions—but especially east—from it.

Adjacent to the Theatre District and the Tenderloin,* the Square offers a colorful montage of life's delights and distresses; and as a downtown shopping area it is equal to any in the world. Moreover, despite the socio-economic problems that have plagued and even destroyed many urban centers since World War II, Union Square has thrived, attracting tens of thousands of locals to shop and promenade every day, and millions of travellers every year.

Theatre in San Francisco enjoys as broad a scope as it does anywhere in the United States. The internationally acclaimed San Francisco Mime Troupe performs its scathing political satires free in parks around The City, where light circus acts and buskers are also likely to be found. Playwrights' workshops, poets' theatres, dance theatres, ethnic performing groups, operetta companies, modern and classical repertory companies: all abound, along with a world-renowned major resident grand opera company, the nation's first ballet company, and similar touring theatres. What San Francisco does not have, however, is a Great White Way akin to New York's Broadway. When I refer to the Theatre District, then, I am speaking of some half-dozen large, Equity-affiliated houses where major resident and touring musicals and plays are staged. These theatres include the Orpheum, on Market Street near Civic Cen-

---

*The Tenderloin: this colorful if (currently) dilapidated district a few blocks southwest of Union Square is a neighborhood in transition, but it is called the Tenderloin for good reason, especially at night.

ter, west several blocks up from where we boarded the Cable Car a few pages back; the Golden Gate, on Taylor just north of Market, also near the Powell and Market turntable; the three theatres on Geary Boulevard immediately west of Union Square: The Geary, the Curran, and, a couple of blocks farther out, the Alcazar, and the Theatre on the Square on Post, and the Marines' Memorial on Sutter. These are the theatres visitors to The City are most likely to see. If you have a deep interest in theatre, and wish to see a wider range of offerings than this Schubert Alley-like strip provides, please consult the "pink pages" magazine of our *Sunday Examiner-Chronicle* newspaper, the various local magazines, the "After Dark" section of the *San Francisco Bay Guardian* and the manager or concierge at your hotel. (See also the Appendices on page *164*).

The block of land that is now Union Square was a gift from Colonel John W. Geary, after whom Geary Boulevard (running alongside the Square in front of Macy's and continuing west virtually to the ocean shore) is named. Col. Geary was The City's first postmaster, and in 1850 was elected its first non-Spanish mayor. He set the land aside, earmarked as a public park, long before any meaningful development took place around it. It is accepted folklore that the Square took its name during the outbreak of the Civil War, when many mass meetings were held in the area, as San Franciscans, who represented all of California at that time, assembled to debate which side the Golden State would take in the conflict. When, by a significant if narrow vote, the decision went for the Federal government and the North's Union armies, a *de facto* christening seems to have taken place.

A brief note is in order here regarding San Francisco's and California's roles in the Civil War. It is not generally known that this part of the country was heavily involved in that epic. The fact that many of the early gold seekers were scions of prominent southern families who established part of San Francisco's first aristocracy bred grave tensions in the state's relationship with the Union. Many passionate confrontations occurred both in The City and in the gold fields, and numerous southern blue bloods returned to their old homes to do battle for the Confederacy. The issue in California was never really that of slavery (slavery was outlawed in California from the beginning); rather, it was States' rights. The territory that was producing millions of dollars in gold and silver annually was most reluctant to offer power over that production to the pointy-headed rascals who held sway in faraway Washington, D.C. It is not germane to elaborate here on California's precise role in the Civil War, save to say that had this state's gold been turned over to the South, some historians believe it would have enabled the Confederacy to buy invincibility, and thus to succeed in its cause.

One of the little-known stories about Union Square, and one of the dearest, is that the tradition of lighting public Christmas trees and making Christmas a day especially for children is said to have begun in the Square well over a century ago, as the odd idea of a little Jewish merchant from London, Joshua A. Norton.

San Francisco has always delighted in eccentrics, and those who march to the beat of a different drummer have always found a home in The City. Of all the colorful and Bohemian characters who made individuality part of the way of life here, none is so typical, beloved, and celebrated as our fond Mr. Norton. His story is well known to everyone familiar with the history of our town, but it always bears retelling; for more than any other person this "loveable old humbug," as Mark Twain affectionately called him, has come to symbolize the noble sense of tolerance and civility that is at the core of the San Francisco spirit.

Norton arrived in San Francisco in the early days of the Gold Rush. Disembarking onto the muddy, tumultuous streets, he immediately set about establishing himself as a shrewd, kind, and honest entrepreneur whose schemes earned him both profits and friends. Indeed, Norton's advice on business and finance was sought by many men of affairs in The City at that time.

Thus, when he unveiled his plans to corner the world's rice market, investors readily came forth with the necessary cash, and the dignified gentleman dreamed grand dreams about the millions his plan would produce. But alas, the ways of the gods are sometimes strange and seemingly perverse. Other, less scrupulous entrepreneurs pulled the rug out from under Norton, and when he had finished paying back his investors after his bubble burst, he found himself destitute.

Rejected, bankrupt, disillusioned, and broken, Norton retreated from The City. Then, one day in the late summer of 1859, he suddenly reappeared on Montgomery Street, wearing a high beaver hat with feathers attached to it, and a uniform that was a comic opera parody of a Latin American military dictator's regalia. With him pranced two mongrel dogs, his beloved pets Bummer and Lazarus. He held a staff of gnarled grapevine wood as a scepter, and displayed ostentatious epaulets on his shoulders. In a word, he had become The Fool: a buffoon, sadly comic, yet utterly likeable. As bemused bystanders watched, Norton sauntered on down the street and into the offices of one of the leading newspapers of the day. He then managed to persuade them —with mild-mannered imperiousness—to print an announcement for all to see proclaiming himself Norton I, Emperor of the United States and (later) protector of Mexico.

In San Francisco, obedience to His Majesty's decree was not only acceptable, it was expected. Not only did the paper print his absurd proclamation, but His Majesty was immediately hailed approvingly by virtually all his subjects. The people, businesses, and government of San Francisco accorded His Gracious Highness every kindness in entertaining the whims of his fanciful empire, feeding him, clothing him, and accepting his chits as imperial currency.

If he was mad, Norton was a noble madman, and many of his royal decrees and ideas were intended to benefit his people. Two testimonials to Norton's vision stand, however, as monuments to his real acumen. It was he who first "commanded" the building of both the Golden Gate and the San Francisco-Oakland Bay Bridges—ideas that were considered preposterous at the time. Norton also believed that there should be an international fraternity of nations working together for world peace and prosperity. If not entirely unique, Norton's dream is worth special note here because in 1945 the United Nations was founded and first headquartered here in The City of St. Francis, a fact that no doubt pleased the spirit of The City's patron saint and Norton's shade as well.

His Majesty's dogs went everywhere with him: to restaurants, theatres, and public meetings; on Cable Cars (which Norton is believed to have ridden on their first day), walks about town, and even to services at Temple Emanu-El and Old St. Mary's Church, in both of which the Emperor worshipped regularly. On the sad day that Lazarus died, the dog was buried at public expense, and thousands of San Franciscans followed it to its grave in what is believed to have been the largest funeral ever held for a dog.

Finally, one January day in 1880, Norton slumped to the street and died in front of Old St. Mary's Church. The people of San Francisco went into great mourning for their beloved Emperor. It was reported that some 30,000 people, including state and civic leaders and assorted dignitaries, marched along with the funeral cortege. The world's press covered the event and published elaborate eulogies. The funeral expenses were borne by the immensely powerful and prestigious Pacific Union Club. Flags were flown at half-mast. When his Imperial Palace, a cheap room in a lodging house on Commercial Street, was cleaned, Norton's Imperial Treasury was found to contain only his dingy uniform, a $2.50 gold piece, $3.00 in silver, an 1823 franc, and 98,200 shares of stock in a worthless gold mine.

But an Emperor such as Norton deserved two funerals. And so, in 1934, members of the Pacific Union Club, along

His Majesty Norton I taking the pleasure of the afternoon air on his bicycle in the 1870's.

with the mayor and a host of other officials and citizens, moved Norton's remains from the private grave in The City to a new crypt in Woodlawn Cemetary in the nearby suburb of Colma. It was a smaller ceremony than he was given the first time, but one befitting the title he claimed, which was chiseled on his handsome new headstone, with no quotation marks or other sense of irony, the inscription being quite clear:

Norton I
Emperor of the United States
and
Protector of Mexico
Joshua A. Norton
1819-1880

***

Shops change owners, change intentions, change locations, and even change customers. For these reasons—as well as to maintain the freedom of my own personal biases—I make mention of relatively few contemporary commercial establishments in these pages, save as directional landmarks, historical points of interest, or as reference to some person, place or event of note.

Around Union Square, the situation is a little different: so many establishments here partake of one or more such exceptions that nearly all should really be listed for your enlightenment. Alas, there are too many; and so, for reasons exactly contrary to those I would usually employ, I mention only a sprinkling of this area's boutiques and outlets. I do not mean by excluding some of the others that they are less worthy of your attention than those included; stop where you like, and see—or buy—what you wish.

Just west of the Square, on Geary, stands another of San Francisco's grand hotels, the Clift. Completed in 1916 in response to demand generated by the 1915 World's Fair, the Clift immediately set its own style for graciousness, which it has maintained to this day. Long a bastion of the conservative wealthy—one previous owner, R.S. Odell, banned the touring company of the risqué rock musical, *Hair,* which played at the Geary Theatre in 1969, because the idea of long hair and exposed human skin did not appeal to him — the hotel has taken, in the 1980s, a chic, modern appearance that does not betray what is best about its traditions. Its restaurants and bars are superb, and it is a minor gallery of work by the Viennese art nouveau master, Gustav von Klimt.

Post Street, from the block west of Union Square down to Montgomery, is among the most enticing places in The City to spend money. In the block west of Powell, on Post Street, the singular high point is John Howell Books, one of the paramount rare book emporia in the world. A few blocks farther west on Post will take you past the Press Club, the Olympic Club, and the ultra-exclusive and powerful Bohemian Club—but unless you are a member of one of these institutions or their out-of-town sisters, or know someone who will bring you as a guest, their delights and secrets will, alas, not be open to you.

On the east side of Powell at Post, you see Saks Fifth Avenue, which needs no introduction. Exactly one block farther east along Post, across Stockton Street, the joyful promenade includes Dunhill's, F.A.O. Schwarz, Gump's, Sulka, Eddie Bauer, Shreve & Co., Elizabeth Arden, and Brooks Brothers. Tiffany's is on Grant, between Post and Sutter, but it may move into the store formerly occupied by Saks, on Grant at Maiden Lane by the time you read this. These are but a few of the many offerings in this part of town.

On the corner of Sutter Street, north up Powell from Saks, stands another of The City's noted hotels, the Sir Francis Drake. Famous for its doormen in Beefeater costumes, The Drake—as locals call it—is resplendent with San Francisco's own sort of grandeur. The grand staircase leading from the lobby may remind you of the stairway at the Grand Opera House in Paris. Upstairs, in the Starlight Room penthouse, dancing to the live band starts about nine in the evening; cocktails begin much earlier.

While you should browse along Post as you see fit, I am going to take the liberty of speaking a little about Gump's, partly because it is home-grown, and partly because there is nothing else quite like it anywhere (except, perhaps, the new Gump's that have opened in Texas and San Diego since 1981). Gump's is where you buy art and elegance; it is a store for people who know quality and can afford it. Founded in 1861, Gump's is a treasure trove of the finest furniture, crystal, silver, and similar sorts of goods; but above all, it is a source of fine Oriental art. The names of some of Gump's departments—The Jade Room; The Silver Room; The Baccarat Room; The Steuben Room; The Oriental Antiques Room—give some inkling that the store purveys what its slogans promise. When Gump's says, "Good taste costs no more," or "Beauty pays dividends," it is speaking from the heart. And if you are unprepared to write out a five- or six-figure check for a rare Ming vase or an original Old Master, you can still find an unusual gift of superior quality here for as little as five or ten bucks.

Near Montgomery, on the south side of Post Street at Number 57, is one of the finest, most unusual private libraries in America, owned by the Mechanics Institute. Unless you are a member—a privilege for which you may apply at the office upstairs—you will not be admitted to this favorite retreat of scholars and master chess players. But even if you are just passing by, you can take a worthwhile moment to step into the rear of the little lobby and look at the lovely, winding staircase and the domed skylight.

At Montgomery, turn north one block and return to Powell Street along Sutter. Here you will find more excellent shops, such as Wilkes Bashford clothiers, Victoria's Secret lingerie, the Academy of Art College, and outstanding art galleries such as the John Pence Gallery, La Ville du Soleil Gallery, and the Stephen Wirtz Gallery. Although this is not the only place in town where major contemporary and antique art is displayed, the Sutter strip has been called the Art Galleries Block, and it surely contains one of the finer accretions of painting, sculpture, and photography to be found anywhere in town. The "500 Sutter" at the corner of Powell and Sutter is a gourmet's delight for lunch or light supper, and also houses a bookstore of foreign language papers, magazines and guides.

Before going on, I should like to make another of my occasional digressions, this one concerning The City's relatively new Neiman Marcus store, located at Geary and Stockton Streets. Up until a few years ago a marvelous pre-Earthquake structure sat on this site. The decision to raze the old City of Paris department store was a battle hard fought against some of San Francisco's ablest preservationists. Mine is not to say whether right or wrong prevailed: the maintenance of historic beauty and the demands of progress ever are at odds. But given that the decision was made as it was, I do have to point out that the most striking feature of the old building, a spectacular art nouveau glass dome superposed over an atrium and grand rotunda, has been preserved and incorporated into the new building. However, I should note that the Philip Johnson exterior design was recently voted the ugliest new building in town. While every choice must have its critics, it seems some part of valor to me to commend Neiman Marcus for incurring the expense and considerable difficulty entailed in preserving this irreplaceable art glass for posterity—and for you, gentle reader, if you've a mind to make a stop. There is a lovely restaurant-cafe on the upper floor of the rotunda.

And now we shall move on. You are still free to shop, of course, at the stores I've mentioned, or at Macy's, I. Magnin, or any of the other large and small shops around. Or you might want to stop for some lunch or a beverage: the options here are many and varied. When you're ready, you can take any of the Powell Cars uphill to Chinatown; you can transfer at California Street from a Powell Car to a California Car and take it downhill to Chinatown's famous Grant Avenue; or you can reach Chinatown by continuing on your Powell Car past California to Jackson Street, and then walking east downhill. In any of these cases, ask your Cable Car Conductor to call out the Chinatown stop for you. On the other hand, if you care to take a short stroll, simply walk back to Post Street, turn north onto Grant Avenue, and continue to the corner of Bush Street two blocks up. That imposing gate in front of you at the corner of Bush and Grant is the official entrance to our next stop, Chinatown.

As I've indicated, Union Square is a shopper's paradise, and if you have shopping on your mind, you owe it to yourself to browse and window-shop throughout this part of town. It is impossible to list all the excellent stores in a guide of this sort, but to help you get started, here are the names, addresses, and telephone numbers of a few of my favorites near the Square.

Elizabeth Arden Salon. Cosmetics. 230 Post Street. 982-3755.

Wilkes Bashford. High fashion clothing for men and women. 336 Sutter Street. 986-4380.

Eddie Bauer. Outdoor and casual wear. 220 Post Street. 986-7600.

Brooks Brothers. Traditional clothing, mostly for men. 201 Post Street. 397-4500.

Alfred Dunhill. Tobacconist, men's wear, executive toys and miscellany. 290 Post Street. 781-3368.

Gucci. Designer fashions. 253 Post Street. 772-2539.

Gump's. Art goods. 250 Post Street. 982-1616.

Liberty House. Department store. Stockton and O'Farrell. 772-2121.

Livingston's. Women's fashions. Main store, 100 Post Street. 362-3060.

Macy's of California. Department store. Stockton and O'Farrell. 397-3333.

I. Magnin. Clothing for men, women, and children. Geary and Stockton. 362-2100.

Joseph Magnin. Clothing for men and women. Stockton and O'Farrell. 772-2505.

Neiman Marcus. Department store. 150 Stockton Street. 362-3900.

Saks Fifth Avenue. Clothing for men and women. 384 Post Street. 986-4300.

F.A.O. Schwarz. Toys, mostly for children. 180 Post Street. 391-0100.

Shreve & Co. Jewelry. Post and Grant. 421-2600.

A. Sulka & Co. Men's clothing. 188 Post Street. 362-3450.

Theodora. Jewelry. Crocker Center Galleria, Post near Montgomery. 398-7464.

Tiffany & Co. Jewelry. 252 Grant Avenue. 781-7000.

Victoria's Secret. Lingerie. 395 Sutter Street. 397-0521.

With all your shopping you are liable to grow hungry or thirsty. Restaurants of all sorts abound around the Square, from quick-stop sandwich shops to haute cuisine dinners. As with the stores, it is neither practical nor possible to list everything that's good, but I offer a few of my personal favorites for your consideration.

Bardelli's Restaurant. 243 O'Farrell Street. 982-0243. **$$
La Bourgogne. 330 Mason Street. 362-7352. ***$$$
Compass Rose. St. Francis Hotel. 397-7000. Drinks.
Mama's in Macy's. 391-3790. *$
Narsai's in I. Magnin. 362-2100. **$ ½
Plaza Restaurant. Hyatt Hotel on Union Square. 398-1234.
    *$ ½
Sears Fine Foods. 439 Powell Street. 986-1160. Breakfast
    and lunch only. ***$
Trader Vic's. 20 Cosmo Place. 776-2232. ***$$$
Le Trianon. 242 O'Farrell Street. 982-9353. ***$$$
Rosebud's English Pub. 370 Geary Street. 433-0813. *$$
Victor's. St. Francis Hotel. 956-7777. **$$$
Donatello. 501 Post Street. 441-7182. ***$$$

Chinatown

Your Cable Car continues up Powell Street from Union
Square and rises over the crest of Nob Hill before descending
into the largest Chinese colony in the western world. China-
town is "the city within The City" where East at last meets
West. Its bustling crowds, and its unusual sights, sounds,
and smells, make it an exciting, mysterious, romantic place
to outsiders; yet, it is also distinctly American and familiar,
despite some differences in manners and life-styles.

San Francisco's Chinatown is a major commercial, histor-
ical and cultural center, located between North Beach and
the Financial District. Residents and businessmen alike are
well aware of their contributions to The City's character, and
they welcome visitors. At the same time, while this quarter
may seem more than a bit exotic or colorful or quaint, it is the
primary business and cultural district for well over 50,000
Chinese-Americans, for whom incessant exposure may some-
times be trying—imagine several million strangers traipsing
around *your* neighborhood every year! And so, your respectful
consideration of their humanity will help create the warmest
possible relations between you and your hosts.

Chinese settlers first arrived in San Francisco before 1849, and, as Oscar Lewis relates, "They were industrious and unassuming, and willing to serve as household servants, or to perform other humble tasks that few of the others would accept under the spur of necessity. In the gold diggings, too, the first Chinese were looked on, if not with approval, at least with tolerance." However, misunderstandings fueled whatever prejudice was innate in the European-Americans toward these people whose culture was unknown (and considered "inferior"). Soon the Chinese condition here was much altered for the worse.

At first, the mistreatment the Chinese suffered was rooted only in social fears. Then the competition of "cheap Chinese labor" came to be seen as dangerous to the white man's job security, and economics exacerbated his fears. Especially on the railroads, where many white workers were already angry with the plutocrats who, they felt, refused to give them a fair share of the enormous profits their work had generated, the Chinese were easy scapegoats. When the Central Pacific Railroad began to import large numbers of Cantonese laborers to lay its rails, a vocal anti-Chinese movement arose. The great depression that spread across the nation in the late 1870s resulted in massive layoffs in the railroads and other California industries, and made the movement violent.

The champion of the white workers' revolution was the fiery Dennis Kearny, whose name, ironically, graces the street that borders Chinatown on the east. Kearny hated not only the Chinese and their employers; he also loathed politicians, bankers, and businessmen in general. In some regards, Kearny and his large band of bigoted followers had good cause to be angry. They were paid scanty wages for backbreaking labor far away from their homes. They were abused by their bosses and frequently cheated by their employers. Finally, they saw those same employers grow increasingly wealthy, increasingly powerful, and increasingly capable of influencing both politics and business to maintain the inequities of their regimes.

Chinatown, corner of Grant Avenue & California Street, c. 1920. Note that the corner & building look much the same today.

Although Kearny's "workingman's revolt" was vigorously bigoted and violent, it was visible enough to be accepted as part of a growing national labor movement that was increasingly national in scope.

In Kearny's context, it is also ironic to note that the first organized workers' strike in The City was staged by Chinese laborers, when a crew of coolies assembling the granite blocks for a Montgomery Street depository suddenly realized that only they could read the ideographically coded markings on the stones, shut the job down, and immediately won a raise. But such a *coup de maitre* was very much the exception, as social attitudes fostered dozens of grossly unjust laws and regulations discriminating against the Chinese, from forced segregation in their ghetto to inequality of education and employment opportunities, to denial of their civil rights as American citizens. Indeed, it was not until the 1960s that the last vestiges of these contemptible rulings were officially laid to rest.

Not all the evils that affected the Chinese resulted from the white man's greed, however. Chinatown bordered the Barbary Coast (see p. *120*) along its entire eastern side, and this marriage gave rise to a fringe area of miserable dens of vice in Chinatown that were as horrific as anything deeper inside the Coast. Most people have heard of opium dens, but in particular, there were numerous Chinese-owned businesses that promulgated the open sale of young Chinese girls as slaves, to be mercilessly abused in prostitution for the exclusive profit of their Chinese owner. The girls, many of whom were as young as ten and twelve years, were paid nothing and fed only enough to keep them alive, were treated like so many cattle by their masters, and were forced to accept any customer regardless of their feelings or his depravity or disease. Once entered into bondage, the average life expectancy for these girls was less than five years.

It turned out to be groups of white civic and religious organizations that endeavored to put a stop to Chinese slavery. Although there were sympathetic Chinese too, these groups at least attempted to rescue some of the girls or offer them care and protection once they escaped, since certain death would follow for any escapee who was recaptured. The noble efforts of the Salvation Army and Mrs. Donaldina Cameron's Presbyterian Home for Girls were brave, since the ruling tongs of that time did not hesitate to kill their enemies.

Today's Chinatown is neither so seamy nor so insidious as the most lurid aspects of its history might suggest. It is a crowded residential district populated largely by immigrants from Hong Kong and Taiwan. While the better-established and more prosperous Chinese move on to the suburbs or more heterogeneous sections of San Francisco and other Bay Area communities, Chinatown remains the cultural center of the whole community, and its principal business and shopping district.

For a variety of cultural reasons, it is unlikely that more than a few dozen white or black men over the years have ever thoroughly understood this "Hong Kong of the West" or its inhabitants, or have been privy to the intricacies of its internal organizations. Fortunately, it is not necessary for the traveller to possess such an intimate knowledge of the district to enjoy it. Simply by exploring the area on foot, and visiting the markets, sampling the restaurants, mixing with the people, and availing oneself of the many offerings in the abundant shops, one can quickly become attuned to its atmosphere, encounter new insights about a still-foreign culture, and even experience the feeling of being, for a time, in a foreign land.

The "differentness" of the East holds many delightful surprises for the Westerner. One of the more amusing can be learning to translate between languages. Chinese writing is a form of ancient, highly sophisticated hieroglyphics, and the spoken language is as distinct from spoken English as the written form is from written English. One translator I know explains that:

> "Sometimes in translating the name of something from English there is an attempt to find a word or words in Chinese which approximate the sound of

the English noun, while at the same time having a meaning in Chinese that conveys what the object is, does, or represents. This can be entertaining, especially when the noun to be translated is the name of a product. Coca-Cola is a good example. What was supposed to result was a phrase translation that more or less meant 'into your mouth—happiness.' However, there is marketing anxiety as the words 'Coca-Cola' themselves translated into Chinese as 'bite the wax tadpole' or 'wax fattened mare' depending on your inflection.

"Other times, the Chinese have chosen to name things of the West with their own words, which, when translated back into English, seem to describe whatever those things are most aptly. When the first Chinese came to San Francisco during the gold rush, they named The City *Gum San Dai Fow,* which translated means Great City of the Golden Hill.

"The hieroglyphic marquee signs on businesses in Chinatown may be phrases expressing something about what the business does, or some kind of prayer for good hopes and wishes, such as 'Place of Abounding Long Life' for a pharmacy, 'Our Growing Prosperity' for a shop, or 'Inside is Happiness' for a restaurant. Also, of course, some businesses are simply named after the family that owns them."

There is as much to see in Chinatown as there is atmosphere to absorb. I suggest you will discover most just wandering on your own; but first, allow me to point out some modern-day highlights you can use as reference points or markers.

Chinatown formally begins at the Chinatown Gate, at the corner of Bush Street and Grant Avenue (see map, p. *28*). Although there was talk for years of building such a gate, the one that stands was not completed until 1970. Two-thirds of the $150,000 expense was borne by San Francisco, one-third by Taiwan. A big parade was held to celebrate the Gate's dedication, with the then Vice-Premier of Nationalist China, Huang Shao-Ku, and then Mayor Joseph Alioto presiding. The plaque hanging above its arch center reads, "The Whole World Is For All The People."

The Chinese Historical Society, at the Portsmouth Square Cultural Center, in the Chinatown Holiday Inn at 750 Kearny Street, has an excellent library and a small museum for use by both researchers and people seeking only general information about Chinese-American history and commerce, and it does offer tours. (See Appendix, p. *161* .) For many people who think of Chinatown as merely a transplanted curiosity or an exotic place to dine, a visit to the Society or one of their tours is an excellent place to begin understanding why China has been a major force in world culture for nearly 5,000 years.

Old St. Mary's Church, at the corner of California and Grant, where the California Street Cable Car passes (see p. *110*), is among the most important historical buildings in San Francisco. Built in 1853, Old St. Mary's was The City's first "cathedral."

Its presence in what was just beginning to be the Chinese ghetto fortuitously afforded its priests and parishoners an excellent opportunity to practice the Christian virtue of charity among the poor and unfortunate who dominated the neighborhood. Operated by the Paulist Fathers today, the church continues these noble traditions, while providing a favored place of worship for numerous Catholics, white, black, brown, and yellow. Among its activities, the church sponsors an all-girl Chinese marching band associated with the church school, which has become internationally famous. And you may recall from the Union Square chapter of this book that Emperor Norton died on the steps of this church in 1880.

Stockton Street, from Clay to Broadway, is Chinatown's market street, and is a high point of any walking tour of this area. Most of the markets are open during normal business hours, Monday through Saturday; Saturday is usually the busiest day of the week. Unless you come from another sophisticated cosmopolitan center such as New York, Tokyo, Paris, or London, and are familiar with the kinds of fare offered in classic, old-style food markets, the wide and

Old Chinatown, 1880's. Note the men's costumes & ques.

unusual selections available in the open markets here, including live frogs, turtles, snails, and a wide assortment of vegetable and sea-animal life, may prove as surprising as it is curious. If some food strikes your fancy in particular, try to find out which restaurants serve it, and go see what you think of it as it is prepared.

Grant Avenue is Chinatown's main street; although there are a few markets here, especially at the north end near Broadway, there are many more shops offering jewelry, silks, furniture, and other fine imported goods. Some of the wares are extremely high-quality, and others are cheap trinkets; usually the differences are apparent in the materials and workmanship, as they are in the prices also. Grant is also the location of most—but not all—of Chinatown's best restaurants. All writers who specialize in gourmet-ing and gourmandizing have their favorites, and a few of my own recommendations can be found on p. *61*. But chefs change as rapidly as tastes, and you will do well to let your palate,

nose, wallet, and intuition guide you to your dinner in this section of town, or you can ask a local resident. As you can see, there is no dearth of places to go and many are among the best Chinese restaurants in the world. Except—there is one restaurant that has become a kind of San Francisco institution; and if I do not recommend Sam Wo's, at 813 Washington, off Grant, for its food, neither do I fault it that way. No, Sam Wo's is really famous as an ethnic restaurant because it is where the scurrilous and internationally famous waiter Edsel Ford Fong will probably insult you in his own peculiar dialect of pidgin English before making you eat what you did not order and assuring you maximum discomfort at a reasonable price. If you have a sense of humor and are mildly adventuresome, eat what the man serves you. If not . . . well, a word to the wise is sufficient, they say.

An important feature of Chinatown's commerce and community is embodied in what Americans call the Six Companies, also known as the Chinese Consolidated Benevolent Association. This far-reaching organization was formed in

Chinatown in the late 1800s as an extension of the tongs that were coming into being; like the tongs themselves, it is a distinctly American Chinese concept.

The first tongs were organized in the gold fields around 1860, as mutual benefit associations that afforded the Chinese aid, protection, and cultural affiliations with other Chinese. They acted to preserve Chinese traditions in the new land, and to oppose the kinds of oppression and discrimination that were becoming prevalent. Some tongs engaged in extortion and other crimes. In conjunction with the tongs, and sometimes as urban extensions of them, Family Organizations and District Associations emerged, both associated with "family store" groups that were and still are controlled by the elders of each clan. The family store groups revolved around the stores and businesses of the fledgling community, and served to orientate new Chinese immigrants. Much of this is still common today.

The Six Companies, so called, it is said, after the six original members, arose as the central organizing committee of all these disparate clubs, groups, and associations, to become the central government of Chinatown, acting under a coordinating board of control made up of representatives from all the other organizations. Among its functions, the Six Companies acts as a *de facto* embassy to Chinese visitors; represents and lobbies for Chinese-American interests; acts as a kind of supreme court to settle disputes between Chinese individuals or organizations within the community; coordinates local fund-raising activities; and operates one of the largest Chinese language schools in America. It also takes a major role in organizing the spectacular Chinese New Year parade, held sometime in late January or February, at the end of the two-week Chinese New Year Festival, which you should absolutely not miss if it coincides with your visit to The City.* *Gung Hay Fat Choy!* That's Happy New Year, in Chinese.

---

*Tentative dates for the next few years: 1984: Feb 2-11; 1985: Feb 20-March 3; 1986: Feb 9-22; 1987: Jan 29-Feb 7; 1988: Feb 17-27; 1989: Feb 6-18; 1990: Jan 27-Feb 10.

There is a great variety of temples in Chinatown representing many sects of Taoism, Buddhism, and other Asian religions. In addition to their functions as places of worship, however, these temples also provide or organize such community services as schools, meeting rooms, dormitories, and meals for the old and poor. Most of the temples are located atop Chinatown buildings, to place them closer to heaven and the gods, and some supposedly represent as many as 17 deities. As you walk through the area, you may see a number of buildings whose appearance is rather plain at street level, but elaborately beautiful at the top; many of these are temple buildings.

The most popular saint or deity in the area is said to be Kuan Yin, a goddess of mercy, or "one who hears prayers." She has a temple dedicated to her in Spofford Alley where tourists are tolerated . . . sometimes. You may also be able to enter the temple at 146 Waverly Place on the second floor. However, almost all the temples in Chinatown, like the various tong benevolent association offices, are emphatically closed to the public. The particular exception to this rule is Buddha's Universal Church on Washington at Kearny. The members of this largest Zen sect center in America built the entire temple, and give regular tours.

Other places of interest do not necessarily keep tourists' hours, but you may find them worth a look. On the fourth floor at 125 Waverly Place is the Tien Hau Temple. It is believed to be the oldest extant Chinese temple building in the United States, and its gold leaf ornamentation makes it one of the more splendid rooms in town.

Sun Yat Sen plotted the Chinese revolution of 1911, against the Empress Tzi Hsi, from 36-38 Spofford Alley. In large measure, this is where the Chinese Republic began. Nearby, at 736-738 Grant Avenue, the now-defunct *Chinese World* newspaper vigorously opposed the Empress. And at the end of Hang Ah Alley, up Sacramento from Grant Avenue, just past Waverly Place, you'll find the *Cathay Times* and *Young China Daily* newspaper offices. The desk at which Sun Yat Sen sat is still in place.

There is a unique Buffano sculpture of Sun in the little St. Mary's Square on Quincy Alley between Pine and California Streets, across from Old St. Mary's Church.

Chinese and Chinese-Americans have contributed much to our history. Dr. Li Po-Tai was one of The City's most famous doctors in the 19th century; his patients included Leland Stanford and Mark Hopkins, and he reportedly saw 150 to 300 patients a day—which earned him $75,000 a year. By 1870, Chinese workers represented 25% of California's miner population; most were independent workers in the beginning, but many banded together to form successful companies later. During the building of the Transcontinental Railroad (1866-69), tens of thousands of Chinese worked under extreme and dangerous conditions for $26.00 per month, without board (the white laborers were paid $35.00 per month plus board). Charles Crocker and Leland Stanford argued eloquently for them before the U.S. Senate as being "indispensable" to railroad construction in the West. However, it cannot be said that their real interest in these people was humanitarian. Farm labor became the major occupation of the Chinese after the 1870s, when at least 75% of the farm work was being done by them. This led many Chinese to distinguish themselves in the agrisciences. For instance, Guey Jones developed a superior variety of rice, leading to a prized California rice industry; and Lue Gim Gong developed improved strains of fruits, the Lue Orange being the most famous. In the early 1900s, Thomas Foon Chew's Bayside Cannery was on a par with Libby and Del Monte. Joe Shoong began the National Dollar Stores chain in 1928.

Most of what you're looking for in Chinatown you'll find just by following your eyes and nose. A few of the sights I discussed in the preceding pages are:

Buddha's Universal Church. Washington and Kearny. 982-6116.
Chinese Culture Center. Holiday Inn, 750 Kearny Street. 986-1822.
Old St. Mary's Church. 660 California Street. 986-4388.

In addition, the Chinese Historical Society of America is located at 17 Alder Alley, off Columbus, next to North Beach (see p. *81*). The telephone number there is 391-1188.

A visit to Chinatown simply cannot be considered complete without lunch or dinner, however, and while it is clearly out of the question to list all the superb restaurants in this part of The City, I offer only a few of my personal favorites to get you started—the first three expensive and the rest ranging from inexpensive to moderate.

Empress of China. 838 Grant Avenue. 434-1345. ***$$$

Imperial Palace. 919 Grant Avenue. 982-4440. ***$$$

Kan's. 708 Grant Avenue. 982-2388. ***$$½

Far East Cafe. 631 Grant Avenue. 982-3245. *$½

Hunan. 853 Kearny Street. 788-2234. (This is the original San Francisco Hunan, whose fame and popularity led to a major nation-wide discovery of this spicy Chinese fare.) ***$

Sam Wo. 813 Washington Street. 982-0596. (Open until 3:00 a.m.) *$

Universal Cafe. 826 Washington Street. 982-7855. *$½

Dick Lee Pastry. 777 Jackson Street. 397-0788. (take-out dim sum). *$

Brandy Ho's Hunan. 217 Columbus Avenue (at Pacific). 788-7527. **$

Li Po Bar. 916 Grant Avenue. 982-0072.

Pot Sticker. 150 Waverly Place. 397-9985. *$

Hang Ah. I-Pagoda Place./Hang Ah Alley (near Sacramento and Stockton). 982-5686. **$

Jackson Cafe. 640 Jackson Street. 986-9717. *$

Shops: As you can see, there is a wealth of shops in Chinatown, ranging from high-class to tourist traps. The best advice is to walk Grant Avenue from Chinatown Gate at Bush north to Broadway (at North Beach), then come back south via Stockton Street. This way, you'll be able to select from most of the major shops and jewelers; but don't hesitate to take some tangents down the side streets.

Russian Hill

For many years both before and after the Earthquake, this hill was home to a remarkable assortment of artists and writers who walked, stumbled, or rode the Cable Car down to North Beach, Chinatown and the Barbary Coast. California's first poet laureate, Ina Coolbrith, entertained many of the literati in her salon here. Mark Twain, Bret Harte, Ambrose Bierce, Frank Norris, and George Sterling were all neighbors in the quarter, though not all at the same time. The Hill takes its name from the Russian colony that lived in the area briefly in the 1860s and 1870s, before moving to the outer Clement Street part of town. Local legend has it that some unknown Russian sailors supposedly died from a

mysterious disease just prior to landing at San Francisco, and were buried here to quarantine the bodies. Actually, there was a proper Russian immigrants' cemetery here.

Today, Russian Hill is known as the choicest urban neighborhood in the United States, according to the research firm of Arthur D. Little. The houses, apartments, and condominiums are mostly attractive, well-appointed and extremely expensive. If you're willing to stroll around a bit, and walk up a couple of steepish hills, you can wander along some

Perhaps the most famous contemporary Cable Car scene: Looking east atop Russian Hill, a Powell & Hyde Car at Lombard Street, "the crookedest street in the world", with Coit Tower & Telegraph Hill in the background.

streets that have an unexpectedly beautiful rural cast, with magnificent vistas between elegant houses hidden under redwoods, screened from passersby by wisteria and bougainvillea—altogether *not* the sorts of sights mentioned in most tour guides to The City.

I suggest you step off the Cable Car, which is now traveling north up Hyde Street, at about Green or Union. The block between these streets, and the following block from Union to Greenwich, are the commercial center of this district. That is, as you can see, there are a couple of art galleries and espresso houses, a few small restaurants, groceries, cleaners—this really is a residential neighborhood, remember. But a stroll up Hyde to the corner of Union will carry you past the original Swensen's ice cream shop and, catty-corner from that, a shop to remember if you're planning a picnic during your stay in the Bay Area, Marcel et Henri Select Meats—a premier charcuterie celebrated 'round the world for its patés. The two popular local spots are Le Petit Cafe, an espresso bar at Green and Larkin, one block west of Hyde, and the Cafe Cine Monde on Hyde near Green, where movie buffs congregate.

The most spectacular Russian Hill views require that you walk east from Hyde, up the hill at any street between Vallejo and Lombard, and seek the little by-ways on the side streets and alleys. Your pleasures here will be the house finch singing in a grove of city trees and the like. The San Francisco Art Institute (not to be confused with the San Francisco Museum of Art, near the Civic Center) is a combination school-studio-gallery where practicing and student artists work and show. Located at 800 Chestnut Street, a few blocks farther north, it is the oldest college of fine arts in the west. Its alumni include Mark Rothko, Ansel Adams, Imogen Cunningham, and others. Throughout the 1000 block of Green Street you will find many elegant (some pre-Earthquake) Victorian townhouses, and the lovely old Engine Company No. 31 firehouse, which is now a private museum and houses, among other artifacts, the original Knickerbocker Engine #5 beloved of Lillie Coit (see North Beach, p. *85*). It is not normally open to the public.

Macondray Lane, up the steps on Taylor between Green and Union, and between Taylor and Leavenworth a few blocks east, is a lovely pastoral stretch; and the walk east, up, over, and down Vallejo Street (one block south of Green) takes you right into North Beach through dramatic vistas and peaceful greenery. Russian Hill Park, between Larkin and Hyde near Lombard, is also a fine place to take the sun and view the Golden Gate.

Russian Hill's most famous attraction is "the crookedest street in the world," that one block of Lombard Street that runs between the Cable Car tracks on Hyde and Leavenworth Street to the east. From the top of this block you can have the classic postcard view of Telegraph Hill and Coit Tower (discussed at greater length in the North Beach chapter of this book, beginning at p. *81*), with North Beach below, and San Francisco Bay as a backdrop. Since so many people pause at this famous intersection, a few brief remarks are in order.

This crooked street was not deliberately built as a tourist attraction. Rather, as you can see, it is so steep that grading a straight road down would have been impossible, and a modified use of the mountaineer's "switchback" was employed. As it happens, this twisty design has encouraged residents to plant lovely flower garden terraces that accentuate the sharp curves and make them graceful. Somewhat to the chagrin of the people who live here, there seems to be an endless parade of sight-seers down Lombard Street today; but everyone seems to tolerate the incursions reasonably well. If you walk or drive the block, please do so with consideration for the residents. Oh, and don't block the intersection at Hyde and Lombard. You are liable to get hit by a Cable Car cresting the hill, if you do.

Near the corner of Hyde and Lombard used to stand an old mansion, long since torn down. But since we're here, I mention it as the scene of what may have been the first art "happening," staged by one of The City's most brilliant, if obscure, artists. In the early days of the twentieth century the Japanese-German artist Sadakichi Harmann was a talent of no small renown. He was an intimate of such other artists as

Claude Debussy and John Barrymore; was well-known as a poet, a painter, and an actor; and was author of the highly-acclaimed classic, *History of American Art*. But of all his visible trades, the one he plied most successfully was that of the eccentric genius who seemed always to be one step ahead of the law or debt collectors.

Harmann once rented the old mansion in question, collected a group of artists, writers, actors, and other parlor philosophers, and prepared the building for use as a center where he could produce dramatic plays as a means of support. His very first production was Ibsen's *Ghosts,* which has a climactic scene calling for a fire. Sadakichi, a devotee of innovative realism, is said to have actually set the mansion on fire to make the dramatic ending of the play very real indeed. It was almost too real, as the flames came close to burning down the house, and many members of the audience barely escaped injury. In spite of the fact that no serious harm resulted, City authorities decided for him that Sadakichi's career as a theatrical producer was over. He went on to other sorts of adventures, including anti-war protests during World War I and a brief Hollywood career with Douglas Fairbanks, but died in Florida during World War II, an ill-remembered hermit.

Enough. Catch the next Cable Car north, and slide with it down the dramatic Hyde Street hill with its peerless view of the Golden Gate to your grand adventures at Fisherman's Wharf and Ghirardelli Square.

A short list to accompany your short stop in this lovely part of The City, where most of your touring should be outside anyway:

Cafe Cine Monde. 1916 Hyde Street. 474-5638.

Marcel et Henri Select Meats. 2000 Hyde Street at Union. 885-6044.

Le Petit Cafe. 2164 Larkin Street. 776-5356.

San Francisco Art Institute. 800 Chestnut Street. 771-7020.

Swensen's Ice Cream. Union and Hyde. 775-6818. (The original outlet for one of San Francisco's best-known ice creams.)

The Fisherman's Wharf Area
including
Ghirardelli Square,
The Cannery
and Pier 39

As you climb down from your Cable Car at the foot of Hyde Street, you face a bewildering assortment of possible next steps. A block to your right is the San Francisco Wine Museum. Ahead of you is the Jefferson Street Pier, the start of The Cannery, and Fisherman's Wharf itself to the east. On your left, directly across the street from Victorian Park and the San Francisco Maritime Museum, is Ghirardelli Square. The Wharf, you see, is an area, a complex of interrelated recreations. I suggest that the best way to get your bearings is to cross Hyde Street and stop for a gentle libation at the Buena Vista bar while I tell you something about the part of town in which you now find yourself. The Buena Vista is a saloon and restaurant that has become something of a legend in its own time, so you might consider this visit one phase of your sightseeing efforts.

The "Bee Vee," as it is often called by locals, has occupied this site since 1895, although the present building was not erected until 1912. In 1952 the Bee Vee made history of a sort by declaring itself to be the first bar in America to serve Irish Coffee. An official plaque on the front of the building attests to the authenticity of the claim.

Needless to say, this bar's name ("Good View") derives from its vantage on the Golden Gate, which has made it a long-standing favorite among residents and visitors alike. Indeed, its popularity is such that cocktail hour can jam the bar severely; if the intimate press of humanity induces claustrophobia in you, time your visit accordingly.

Presuming the fog is not in, the Bee Vee's windows give onto the Bay, the Golden Gate Bridge, and, to the north, a few of the wealthy communities of southern Marin County. Sausalito, the most famous and perhaps the most picturesque of these towns, is the clutch of buildings clinging to the

hillside just to the right of the far north end of the Golden Gate Bridge. The lovely, tall hill you can see in the short distance beyond Sausalito is Mount Tamalpais, known locally as Mount Tam. More than 2500 feet high, it is the tallest peak in the immediate Bay Area. Like much of Marin County, including the breathtaking Muir Woods (see Appendix, p. *158* , for tour information), Mount Tam is preserved in its natural state as part of the National and State Parks trusts. Its name derives from the local Indian words meaning "bay" and "mountain."

Continuing your gaze eastward, you can glimpse part of the exclusive community of Tiburon, just left of what appears to be another green mountain. This hill, situated behind the rock-like fortress of Alcatraz Island, is Angel Island, another preserve of the Parks system. It has a yacht harbor on its north side, excellent hiking trails and picnic sites, and herds of friendly wild deer wandering about. Angel Island is exactly one square mile, 640 hilly acres, and has been an important feature of the Bay since at least the time

The modern day "line up" to board — this scene being at the Victoria Park terminal of the Hyde Line near Ghirardelli Square.

Manuel de Ayala sailed these waters in 1775. Richard Henry Dana mentions the island in *Two Years Before the Mast,* and it has been the scene of many nineteenth century hot-tempered duels of private import, as well as having been used by the United States military forces as a major staging area for troops during both World Wars. It has also been used as a United States Quarantine Station, and in its most repugnant period, as the major Pacific Immigration Station at the turn of the century—the West Coast counterpart to New York's Ellis Island. You can reach Angel Island by ferry boat for a relaxing day- or half-day-long outing. I suggest you bring a picnic lunch, because there are no food services available there. (See Appendix, p. *160* , for further information.)

From your window in the Bee Vee, Alcatraz Island sits to the right and just in front of Angel Island. It is the most famous island in the Bay, its name long-associated with the maximum-security Federal prison that once operated there. The name, Alcatraz, is said to come from an obsolete Spanish slang word for pelicans, which supposedly meant "ugly birds"—perhaps not an inapt appellation considering the infamous jailbirds who have roosted in The Rock's confines.

Before its long, illustrious career as host to some of America's best-known criminals, Alcatraz Island had a history of other uses by the Federal government. In 1854 it became the first lighthouse station in the Bay; in 1859 the island was taken over and a fort established by the United States Army, with cannon installed to command the entrance to the Bay. But it was not until the island was formally converted into a Federal Prison, in 1933, that it gained its notorious reputation as the place where Al Capone, "Machine Gun" Kelly, Richard Stroud (the bird man), and other nefarious villains were sentenced to languish in its "escape-proof" confines.

As a prison, Alcatraz was closed down in 1963. It reopened in 1972 as a museum, another part of the Golden Gate National Recreation Area. In the interim, from the fall of 1969 until the summer of 1971, The Rock was claimed and occupied by members of the American Indian Movement, protesting their people's treatment at the hands of the United States government. At present, the government's plan is to keep and repair only the main buildings, and to continue using them as a museum.

If you want to find out what it feels like to sit in a solitary confinement cell, and learn some colorful tales about real escapes, riots, inhumanity, murder, and other incivilities, the Park Service offers a good tour (for information, see Appendix, p. 159). All the other buildings on the Island are slated for removal, and the land, as part of the Golden Gate National Recreation Area, is slated to become a public park and bird sanctuary, which is not, I think, an unhappy conclusion. However, the current, most intriguing redevelopment idea for Alcatraz—and my favorite—is "The Phoenix Process" project of the San Francisco Medical Research Foundation: a grand proposal for the conversion of the island into a wholistic health, education and creative arts center. Curious? Call them at 457-0730.

As you saunter out of the Bee Vee you are in the Wharf Area, which includes all those sites I mentioned in this chapter's first paragraph. This area is considered by some people to be "for tourists"—a pejorative notion that suggests it is nothing but an exploitative face of jaundiced commercialism. While there surely are some crass examples of that force in the complex, this is also one of the most colorful, attractive, and unusual shopping and dining centers in the nation, with a setting no less enviable than its best contents. As the Eiffel Tower, the Roman Colosseum, the Tower of London, and other attractive sub-wonders of the world frequently are of genuine and legitimate interest to people—the profit motive apart—so also is the Wharf Area.

Turn up Beach Street as you leave the Bee Vee and head west one block to Larkin Street. You will come to the celebrated Ghirardelli Square. On our side of the street you may wish to pause at some of the shops and art galleries. Across the street you can see lines of portable sidewalk stalls where some of The City's notarized (not notorious; these vendors are licensed) street artists work in front of the Cable Car turntable in and about Victorian Park. City Hall issues permits to artists such as these, allowing them to entertain you, display their work, and earn a livelihood thereby. Many of the wares displayed here are of good quality; and even if you are only window-shopping, the street artists are worth your consideration because such activities as theirs are not to be seen on the streets in most other American cities.

When you're ready, proceed through the shops and restaurants of GHIRARDELLI SQUARE. In the Gold Rush days, Domenico Ghirardelli came to San Francisco from his native Italy by way of Peru, and founded the Ghirardelli Chocolate Company. In 1892, his sons took over the family business, and soon thereafter built the plant much as we see it today, housing offices, the factory, and other essential structures. The clock tower, copied from the style of Chateau Blois in France, instantly became a popular City landmark.

In the early 1960s the Chocolate Company moved to new, larger facilities in the suburb of San Leandro, and for a while this complex was a collection of largely vacant buildings. Then, in 1962, a prominent San Francisco family headed by William Matson Roth bought the complex and turned the premises into what was, at the time, a shopping center unique in the country. The first section of the restoration opened in 1964, the remainder in 1968. It immediately became a nationwide model for restoring and recycling worthwile old structures. Although the Matson-Roth family is no longer associated with this complex, the tradition they established continues.

Today, there are some ninety tenants in the Ghirardelli Square complex, offering a splendid variety of consumer goods, art, and food from all over the world. The Square is full of excellent restaurants, including Modesto Lanzone's, The Mandarin, Paprikas Fono, The Portofino Cafe, and Maxwell's Plum. Within the complex you can buy a quarter-pound of fine writing paper, a crystal goblet, a futuristic clock, an imported peasant sweater, a bar of herbal soap, today's best-selling book, a toy for the kids—even a Ghirardelli Chocolate Ice Cream Sundae. If you find you're making a lot of purchases here, or a few large ones, ask for receipts and ask the cashiers to hold your purchases until you're ready to go home; then take a taxicab instead of the Cable Car to your hotel. (For the telephone numbers of taxicabs in The City, see Appendix, p. *165* .) A guide map to the Square is available at the information booth on the main level.

Across the street from the northwest corner of the Square, at 680 Beach Street, corner of Polk, is the San Francisco Maritime Museum; to its right as you face it, on the Hyde Street Pier, is the San Francisco Maritime State Historical Park. Both are delights if you have but a passing interest in things nautical. The research library and intriguing collections of photographs, rare ships models, hardware, historical displays, and historical ships are among the best of their kind anywhere in the Western United States.

The Maritime Museum also owns and operates several historic ships berthed in this area. Among the ships at the Hyde Street Pier is the paddle tug *Eppleton Hall,* which museum trustee Scott Newhall bought in England in the late 1960s, restored, and sailed home as her captain. The famous *Balcutha* is tied up at Pier 43, just east of the Wharf complex, and is open to the public.

Walking east past the Cable Car turntable and Victorian Park, the huge, red brick complex before you is THE CANNERY. In a sense, this shopping-entertainment-dining center is the sequel to Ghirardelli Square. Originally a canning factory, the structure fell vacant in 1963 when its owner, the Del Monte Fruit Co., moved to larger facilities outside The City. It was purchased by San Francisco attorney Leonard Martin, and converted to its present use.

In The Cannery's courtyard, amid flower carts and olive trees, street musicians and entertainers perform, artists paint, patrons stroll or lounge on benches and at sidewalk cafes. Operatic performances, and Renaissance and chamber music concerts, are scheduled here periodically, and are always free to the public—although, if a hat is passed, a donation is the customary response. There are some fifty shops, restaurants, and galleries in The Cannery, as various as those in Ghirardelli.

The most famous of The Cannery's many eateries is the Ben Jonson, with its magnificent, authentic seventeenth century English furnishings and wood panelling. What you see in this tavern-restaurant is for real. The hundred-foot-long hall of the pub area was originally the Long Gallery of Albyn's Hall, given to Sir Thomas Edmonds by Her Majesty Queen Elizabeth I when he was Ambassador to France. The three grand Elizabethan dining rooms upstairs are likewise authentic. This priceless collection of artifacts was part of the treasure trove of William Randolph Hearst brought to the United States to furnish his colossal San Simeon home, about 200 miles south of San Francisco. Like other shipments of Hearst's goods, however, these pieces wound up in some warehouse gathering dust until the restaurant's original owner uncovered them.

Speaking of original owners, Ben Jonson's management has changed more than once during the time I spent working on this book, and the food and service have ranged from excellent to atrocious, so I suggest you check a current restaurant review. However, the majestic decor makes a quaint atmosphere for cocktails.

Across the street from The Cannery, on the south side of Beach Street between Hyde and Leavenworth, near where the latter crosses Columbus, you will find the San Francisco Wine Museum, housing an educational exhibit on the arts of wine making, and a fine collection of rare and antique glassware.

The Powell-Mason Cable Car line is where you're headed, in a slightly oblique way. It is located near the eastern end of Fisherman's Wharf, pretty much in the direction you've been moving. But before going home to your hotel, there is a major visit to make.

East on Jefferson Street, about two blocks farther on, stands FISHERMAN'S WHARF itself. The heart of this second-most-visited visitor attraction in America after Disneyland, the Wharf itself is a colorful mixture of famous old restaurants and unsung new ones, fine merchandise and tasteless gimcrackery, rides and arcade games, tour boat docks, and, of course, the cove in which the fishing boats berth that give this area its name. These fishing boats are not just props. Although much has changed at the Wharf in the past hundred years, the fishing fleet still goes out, even though it is much smaller and far less romantic today than in the past. Indeed, a number of the boats are for hire; and if you're prepared to be aboard very early in the morning, fishing for salmon outside the Golden Gate can be an exhilerating experience. For more information on such charters, though, you should call the phone numbers prominently displayed on the masts of those boats that are rentable, and discuss your needs with the captains. If you do go out onto the ocean, dress warmly—it is much colder than you think, standing on shore in the sun.

The immigrant Italians were the first to do their commercial fishing from this part of town as early as the 1850s. In the nineteenth century, and even into the twentieth, the Italian fishing fleets with their romantic boats with lanteen sails were common on The Bay. Alas, they are now a forgotten memory. The area then also functioned as a kind of resort spot—although nothing like what it is today—with a variety of short-lived establishments thriving and dying throughout the second half of the nineteenth century. It was in these years that a businessman named Harry Meiggs developed Meiggs' Wharf, considered the precursor to Fisherman's Wharf; and Meiggs Wharf was the site of one of the most unusual establishments in early San Francisco Bohemia.

The place was called The Old Cobweb Palace. It was a sort of combination bar-zoo-restaurant-kindergarten-curio shop that was known as an intriguing delight in the pre-Earthquake era. This menagerie-drinking establishment was run by an aging eccentric named Abe Warner, who served from the rear room of his small, ramshackle building only the very finest of imported cognacs, wines, and ales, along with fresh crab and clam concoctions. Because of the high quality of his liquors, connoisseurs frequented his place; and they could bring their children, because not only was Warner fond of little people, but also his extraordinary collection of live monkeys, bears, parrots, and other animals would keep the tykes amused for hours. Warner had decorated his place with a vast accumulation of curios brought to him by sailors from all over the world, and these were "piled indiscriminately everywhere, and there were boxes and barrels piled with no regard whatever for regularity. This heterogenous conglomeration was covered with years of dust and cobwebs, hence its name." So recalls Clarence E. Edwords, writing of the place.

Going to the Wharf to eat probably grew out of the custom of fishermen's wives operating small kitchens—crab pots and the like—on the spot to cook a visitor's purchases, and to provide a good hot meal for their men after a cold day at sea. Fisherman's Wharf as we know it, however, did not begin to develop until the 1930s, when the first of the big restaurants were established. Then, with the thousands of G.I.'s passing through The City during World War II, the area became world-famous.

The Alioto family, which gave The City a recent, highly colorful mayor, owns the largest number of restaurants down here; and there are many others, of which Scoma's, Pompeii's Grotto and A. Sabella's are among the old favorites. Of course, there is also shopping of all sorts, and just beyond the crowds, some good views of the Bay.

The Wharf is constantly changing and growing. Most recently, Warren Simmons constructed a $35 million low-rise building complex just east of the established Wharf, known as PIER 39. It houses some twenty-two restaurants, one-hundred-ten shops, and a boating marina, all with turn-of-the-century themes. There are also arcade games, dodgem cars, and special entertainers. Pier 39 is located a few blocks northeast of the Bay and Taylor terminal of the Mason Street Cable Car you will take back to or toward Market Street, but it is not a long walk, and there are shuttle buses that run to it as well. Although a number of the restaurants at Pier 39 are good, one must be singled out because it is so remarkably unlike any of the others; that is the Eagle Cafe.

Until the development of Pier 39, and with it the multi-level parking facilities across from it, the old Eagle Cafe sat immediately over on the south side of the road. It was a richly earthy place, frequented by longshoremen, fishermen, and sailors. It served decent food at fair prices.

With all the development going on around it, it was obvious that sooner or later the Eagle was going to have to go. And go it did. But, like that other mythical bird we've met so often in San Francisco, it reappeared—this time in the belly of the complex that had swallowed it. The Eagle was cosmetically altered, but at heart it is very much the same old bird. It opens early for the boatmen who need hot wake-up coffee, it does not serve haute cuisine, and in an era that sometimes seems over-dandified, it is a refreshing reminiscence of The City's rough-and-tumble roots.

Another unique watering hole here is Turk Murphy's Earthquake McGoon's, where Turk Murphy himself presides over the entertainment at one of the world's most famous Dixieland Jazz clubs.

It has been said that between Ghirardelli Square, The Cannery, Fisherman's Wharf, and Pier 39, there is nothing you cannot buy, do, or eat that is generally available in the

United States. I don't know exactly how far such an outrageous statement can be tested, but feel free to give it a try if you are so inclined. Remember, there are about 400 different stores, arcades, museums, and restaurants located within these four complexes, and they are designed to cater to your desires. Instead of attempting to list some of my personal favorites among the numerous shops in this area, I'll provide you with three central telephone numbers for information.

The Cannery. 771-3112.
Ghirardelli Square. 775-5500.
Pier 39. 981-7437.

Fisherman's Wharf itself has no central clearing number.

As I've indicated, there are scores of culinary delights of varying quality available along this mile or so of promenade, from fast food to leisurely dining. And for food, I will provide you with a few outstanding leads.

The Buena Vista Cafe (the Bee Vee). 2765 Hyde Street. 474-5044. *$

Ghirardelli Square:
Gaylord's Indian Restaurant. 771-8822. **$$
The Mandarin. Chinese. 673-8812. **$$
Maxwell's Plum. 441-4140. (The gaudiest restaurant west of Maxwell's Plum in New York.) *$$
Modesto Lanzone's. Italian. 771-2880. **½ $$
Paprikas Fono. Hungarian. 441-1223. *$$

Fisherman's Wharf:
Pompeii's Grotto. 776-9265. *$$
A. Sabella's. 771-6775. *$$
Scoma's. 771-4383. **$$

Pier 39:
The Eagle Cafe. 433-3689. *$
Turk Murphy's (Earthquake Magoon's). 986-1433. (Dixieland Jazz club.)

THE POWELL-MASON LINE
Bay and Mason

When you're through browsing at the Wharf, wend your way to the Mason Street Cable Car turntable at the corner of Bay and Taylor Streets, a couple

of blocks south of the Wharf complex, near the large Cost Plus Imports complex, Ginsburg's Irish Pub, and the North Point Theatre (see map, p. *80*).

The Powell-Mason is the other half of the Powell-Hyde line you ride to the Wharf on. They merge—or diverge, depending on your direction of travel—in the residential section of Chinatown, at the Cable Car Barn just off Nob

Contemporary photo of Fisherman's Wharf showing the fishing boats & two of the area's most famous restaurants.

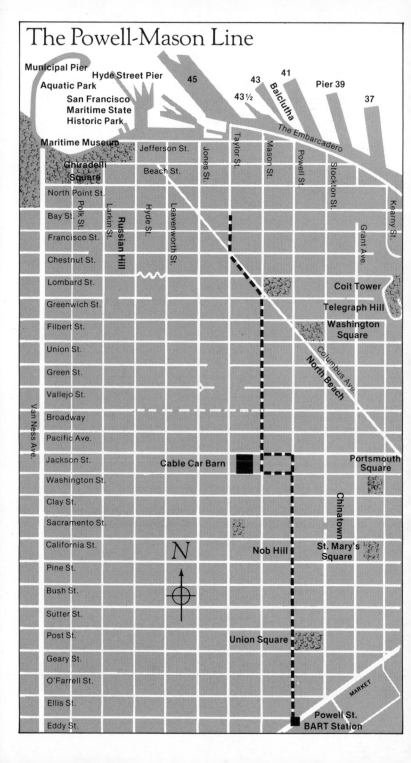

Hill. The Mason line will return you to that spot, and from there back to Powell and Market. Along the way it passes a few places you won't want to miss.

One such place to keep in mind is the Cable Car Powerhouse and Barn, including the excellent Cable Car Museum, which I mentioned to you in "The Last Magic Carpet," on p. 22 . To visit this dormitory for all San Francisco's Cable Cars, and to have your Cable Car questions answered on the spot by the Museum's helpful and expert staff, disembark in the block on Mason between Jackson and Washington, where the two Powell Street Cable lines come together. If you think you might become too enthralled with your ride to remember where your stop is, just tell your Cable Car Gripman or Conductor where you want to go, and he or she will call out the stop for you. Note also that with the proper ticket or transfer, you can get off or on here without having to pay another fare. Check with your Conductor or Gripman.

But even before you reach the Cable Car Barn you will come to my own favorite part of San Francisco, North Beach.

North Beach
The Last Bohemia

The most cosmopolitan downtown city neighborhood in America, San Francisco's North Beach is legendary for the historic attractions, notable people and avant-garde movements that got their start or came to prominence in its oddly nurturing streets. Italian by heritage and Bohemian by nature, North Beach has been compared with New York's Greenwich Village, London's Soho, the Left Bank of Paris and various other hotbeds of radical art and culture; but none of the comparisons has really been apt. North Beach is unique.

Situated between Chinatown and the Financial District on the south, and Fisherman's Wharf on the north, North Beach is the "secret" must-see area of The City for those who want to begin to experience it.

There is no end to the list of names of people who have called North Beach home, or wished they could. During The City's Golden Era, Mark Twain, Robert Louis Stevenson, Ambrose Bierce, Jack London, Oscar Wilde, Rudyard Kipling, and their ilk knew these streets. Later on, it was Gertrude Stein, Isadora Duncan, Alexander Calder, Dashiell Hammett, Eric Hoffer, Rudolph Valentino, Robinson Jeffers and Cecil B. DeMille who, at least briefly, sojourned here. In the second San Francisco Renaissance during the 1950s and 1960s, North Beach was home base for poets such as Lawrence Ferlinghetti, Allen Ginsberg, Gary Snyder, Jack Kerouac, and Michael McClure, who launched the Beat Generation. At the same time, the celebrated sculptor, Benjamino Buffano, was doing some of his most innovative work here, and impressario Enrico Banducci used his night club, the Hungry I, to inaugurate the careers of entertainers such as Lenny Bruce, Woody Allen, Mort Saul, Barbra Streisand, Bill Cosby, Flip Wilson, Dick Gregory, and The Limelighters. The characters who populate North Beach's history are as colorful as the area itself, and our national culture would be far poorer had not its special atmosphere touched us all to the heart.*

The original Hungry I was owned by Big Daddy Nord, the self-proclaimed King of the Beatniks, and located in the basement of the now-defunct and razed International Hotel. Its appellation presumably stood for the hungry id, or hungry intellectual, depending on whose explanation satisfied your ear. Banducci acquired the business and its name from Nord, and sold it to others after the flowering of his particular renaissance had ended. He now operates a famous, fashionable sidewalk cafe and restaurant, Enrico's, set amidst the gaudy glitter of Broadway's topless clubs. However, he has no connection with the topless bar that is presently called the Hungry I.

In The City's earliest days, the waters of the Bay lapped against Goat (now Telegraph) Hill, and this district was

---

*Some footnotes to history. The word "beatnik" is generally acknowledged to have been coined by San Francisco's celebrated columnist, Herb Caen.

Lotta Crabtree in the full bloom of her youth.

literally the "north beach" of the original town plaza at Portsmouth Square. Scant attention was paid to the wharf facilities at Clark's Point at the foot of Broadway, or to the potato field and small dairy farm that were the other highlights of the area.

The first settlers on the slopes of this hill were gold seekers from Latin America and the eastern United States, who built a tent city here, then added scattered houses near the waterfront. From this haphazard accretion of transients' domiciles grew the infamous Barbary Coast (see p. *120*) and, later, Fisherman's Wharf, Chinatown, and the Financial District (see pp. *67, 49, 128*).

Finally, the houses of a neighborhood began to appear in the valley between Telegraph and Russian Hills. (Irish immigrants built some homes on Telegraph Hill soon after the Gold Rush, before making the old South of Market Street area their pre-Earthquake district; and there were numerous French and Mexican and even Hindu settlers here as well.) However, it was the Italians who *made* North Beach, and it is the Italians who are still the characteristic ethnic group here, despite the recent influx of Chinese. At one time, this neighborhood was virtually all Italian. Among the Italian-Americans who were known in this part of town were A.P. Giannini, founder of the Bank of America; Samuele Sebastiani and Robert Mondavi, who founded some of California's great wineries; and Gaetano Merola, founding director of the San Francisco Opera. But notable as these names are, they but hint at the fabulous reach of the great Italian-American heritage that developed in North Beach. The people and their contributions to San Francisco and America are simply too extensive even to list in this volume. If your curiosity demands some satisfaction, you can begin by visiting the little Italian Museum, here to enlighten visitors (see Appendix, p. *167*). Also, there is the Museo- Italo *398-2660* (see Appendix, p. *161*).

Telegraph is San Francisco's most famous Hill after Nob. As with the famous Coit Tower that rises like a quaint silo from its peak and is its special monument, Telegraph Hill's crest embodies its own bright story.

As I mentioned, Telegraph Hill was originally known as Goat Hill, and yes, herds of goats did graze its slopes briefly during the mid-nineteenth century. In 1850, a semaphore-type marine telegraph was constructed on its summit to signal to the hoards of new settlers what nature of ship and cargo was arriving through the Golden Gate. The name Telegraph Hill became firmly established among the populace, even though the telegraph station itself remained in place for only about three-and-one-half years.

Following the chaos occasioned by the Gold Rush, many homes and a number of other, unusual, structures were erected on the Hill. The most famous of these was The German Castle and Telegraph Hill Observatory—a huge, wooden structure resembling a baronial manor built by a man named Layman in the 1880s. He intended to make his complex into a major resort and tourist attraction. A Cable Car line was built up to the castle, where mounted knights in shining armor staged mock jousting tournaments for a bemused public. After years of effort the entire venture was deemed a failure. The castle remained a curiosity until it was claimed by fire shortly before the 1906 Earthquake.

In case you wonder why the east side of Telegraph Hill looks as if it has been cut away, it has. From the Gold Rush days until well into the twentieth century, aggressive stone quarrymen blasted away at the side of the Hill with no evident concern for either the Hill or the people who lived on it. Fortunately, such activity has long been stopped by now, and the east side of the Hill has become home to fine decorator showrooms, art galleries, antique warehouses, luxury condominiums, and low-rise office complexes.

Telegraph Hill's famous Coit Tower was completed in 1933 with funds left to The City by one of our most beloved characters, Lillie Hitchcock Coit, or "Fire-belle Lillie," as she was known in her day. The unusual monument (open to the public, with an observation deck on top—see Appendix, p. *157*) was the result of her bequest to honor the memory of San Francisco's original volunteer fire department, and to somehow add beauty to the place she loved. As a colorful eccentric, Lillie ranks right up there with Emperor Norton.

But she was no crack-brained crazy. Unconventional, yes; a daring individualist, certainly; but her spirited nature was that of a bright, clever, well-bred lady who was not afraid to be herself when willful and independent behavior in a woman was considered aberrant and socially unacceptable.

During the early years, when San Francisco was plagued by fires, The City had no fire department as such; it depended, rather, on the services of several privately-run volunteer fire-fighting companies. It was considered a great honor, as well as a civic duty, to serve in or aid these companies.

Lillie was a child when she arrived here, and her parents took up residence at the historically fashionable Oriental Hotel, then next door to the building that housed the celebrated volunteer Knickerbocker Engine Company Number 5. Lillie was soon taken with the drama and excitement of following No. 5 to the flames whenever the fire bells sounded. Chasing No. 5 became the young girl's passion and her pastime, and soon she was made an honorary member of the company—an honor she cherished until her death in 1929. Dressed in a Knickerbocker uniform and a red handkerchief, it is said she would sit in her window and cheer the men on whenever No. 5 was called out to do its duty, and that she always left a light burning in her window until the fire-fighters returned.

During the American Civil War, Lillie was an ardent supporter of the Southern cause. Fearing for her well-being in this Union city, her father, a high-ranking military doctor at the Presidio, sent both Lillie and her mother to Paris. While there, Lillie acted as official translator of all documents sent by the Confederacy to the French government, and so charmed the French aristocracy that she was invited to attend all court functions.

After the Civil War, Lillie came home, retired from politics, and married Benjamin H. Coit, a stock exchange executive. Far from retiring from the social scene, however, the cigar-smoking, poker-playing, shrewd, outspoken Lillie became the belle of San Francisco. As a writer, an equestrian, and a prominent social figure, Lillie Hitchcock Coit was a living example of the San Francisco spirit. She was even involved in a murder scandal, but that is another story.

When you visit the Tower that bears her name, be sure to see the murals that decorate the interior walls on the main

A young Lillie Hitchcock Coit in her Engine No. 5 uniform.

floor before you take the elevator to the observation deck for a view of the Bay Area that is truly unparalleled. These murals, the first commission under the Federal government's Public Works of Art Project during the Great Depression, depict California life, history, and business. They are the work of some two dozen noted artists of the day, and instigated a surge of fresco painting all across the country.

In the 1920s, from his laboratory on Green Street at the base of Telegraph Hill, Philo T. Farnsworth broadcast the world's first television picture. But for most of us today, it was in the 1950s that North Beach became world famous as a center of Bohemia. It was the birthplace of the Beat Generation, and of many important social, political, and artistic movements that have influenced western culture ever since.

In 1953, Lawrence Ferlinghetti opened the City Lights bookstore and publishing company, both of which became centers for the growing counter-culture. The bookstore is still located at 261 Columbus Avenue at Adler Place Alley, just down from the topless joints of Broadway, next door to Vesuvio's and across the street from Spec's—two of the premier watering holes for local artists, writers, and musicians. City Lights was the first all-paperback bookstore in America, and the place the Beats came to browse, socialize, and exchange ideas. To this day, the publishing imprint signifies the best in innovative literary publishing in America.

But while City Lights Books became a networking center for the intellectual community, it was along upper Grant Avenue, between Broadway and Filbert Streets, that the newly arrived Beats, and the curious others, headed at the height of the Beat Movement. Along the Avenue, dozens of "Bohemian" shops, art galleries, restaurants, and coffee houses opened in the late 1950s and early 1960s, including the Coexistence Bagel Shop, the Coffee Gallery, the Black Cat, and the MDR. Today, only the Caffe Trieste, the Savoy-Tivoli, the Old Spaghetti Factory, and a few other such establishments survive from those days. They are still Bohemian gathering places and well worth the visit.

Although the Beat Movement is now history, the Avenue

is still quite Bohemian in flavor. And now with a bit of an Oriental accent, too. Lately, indeed, the area has been enjoying a real renaissance. For example, North Beach has surely become a prime contender for coffee house capital of America. There are presently something like two dozen thriving cafes within a six-block area, which is certain to be one of the highest concentrations of caffeine anywhere in the world. The free and open flavor of the coffee house scene here has raised the Bohemian life-style to the level of an art. "Hanging out," an entertaining, delightful custom of cosmopolitan civility almost unknown in most American cities, is expressed nowhere so well as in the Italian espresso houses of North Beach. Somehow, they inspire an informal, convivial sense of brotherhood among the people who frequent the shops and converse casually. In the friendly Italian atmosphere the charm becomes as genuine as it is relaxing. Although, as always, you will find my own favorite spots listed at the end of this chapter, you should certainly plan to stop and have an espresso or a cappucino or a latte or whatever else pleases your palate at one or more of these historic cafes.

Today's North Beach is a region of contrasts, as an increasing number of people from non-Italian ethnic backgrounds—particularly Chinese—move into the area. Nonetheless, it still maintains the charm of its unique Italian character, accepting diversity as it always has seemed to do. Marco Polo would have understood and loved today's North Beach. Many North Beach professional associations are working to preserve the historic heritage of North Beach—a heritage essential to San Francisco's well-being.

There are two parts to modern North Beach: the old residential and commercial section whose center is Washington Square Park at the foot of Telegraph Hill, and the clutch of strip show clubs along Broadway and Columbus. These latter are leftovers from the big topless fad that started here in the 1960s. They are neither as bawdy nor as fulfilling as some The City has seen in its raunchier days. They are pricey by the time you've bought your drinks, and, quite frankly, may leave you disappointed in more ways than one. Some, such as The Condor Club at the corner of Broadway and Columbus, may be worth a stop simply for their historic value; this is where Carol Doda and her famous silicon implants held sway for two decades. Also along the Broadway strip, however, are several excellent restaurants and clubs.

Finocchio's offers one of the world's most famous female-impersonator revues each night in the building above Enrico's sidewalk cafe, itself a favorite gathering spot for people who like to see and be seen. Tommaso's pizza emporium, on Kearny just down from the Broadway intersection, offers excellent deep-dish pizza, sauteed zucchini, and other delectables. Up from Tommaso's across Broadway is the renowned Vanessi's, where roast beef and canelloni top an excellent, varied menu. Currently, there are punk rock music clubs, stage shows, game arcades, an Arab market, belly dancing, a strip show for women featuring comely young men, and an all-night disco, the Palladium, not to mention the topless bars featuring attractive women. On New Year's Eve the intersection of Broadway and Columbus is San Francisco's Times Square, full of revellers ringing and singing in the New Year. At the Tosca Cafe, near Spec's and across Columbus from City Lights and Vesuvio's, you can hear opera on the jukebox while sipping a hot chocolate and brandy version of cappucino. Indeed, from the ridiculous to the sublime, this part of North Beach exudes some of the best and worst of the spirit that has made San Francisco.

The other North Beach—the less prurient, less commercial one—is the neighborhood spreading out from Washington Square Park at Columbus, Union, Stockton, and Greenwich Streets. If you disembark your Mason Cable Car at Union and Mason and walk east, you'll find yourself at the Park itself in slightly more than one block. On your way, you'll pass the Intersection theatre, where avant-garde theatrical works are performed in what used to be a church. Facing the Park is the gorgeously spired Church of Saints Peter and Paul, which was completed in 1922, replacing the church that burned in 1906. It is administered by Salesian priests as the spiritual center of the Italian community. It is said that when Cecil B. De Mille was filming the original, silent screen version of *The Ten Commandments* he draped the steel framework of the towers with backdrops for some of his scenes.

From the Square, there are vast numbers of restaurants, bars, cafes, and stores you may want to visit. Among the best-known is the Washington Square Bar and Grill, on Powell off Union, just past the small triangle across Columbus from the Park. The B & G is a popular hangout for some of The City's most famous journalists and authors. The bar is always active, and the anchovy mayonnaise that accompanies the deep-fried calamari is unusual. Founded in 1886, the Fior d'Italia, across from the Park on Union Street, is one of San Francisco's most prominent Italian restaurants. The #39 bus, that stops at the corner of Columbus and Union, will take you up to Coit Tower if you don't relish walking. (Remember, you can transfer from a Cable Car to a bus and vice versa; ask your Conductor or Gripman).

A proper tour of North Beach, starting from the Park, more or less demands that you walk in an ever-widening spiral, in order to miss nothing. But if your time is limited, walk on up Union Street past the Park one block, and turn right on Grant. As I mentioned, this is the street that saw the start of the Beat Movement in the 1950s, and where the "flower children" of the 1960s came before branching out to the celebrated Haight-Ashbury district across town, and Berkeley across the Bay; from there to influence the world and an entire generation.

Grant is one of those streets that is too rich to describe adequately; but since it is only a few blocks from Union south to Broadway, you can walk it very easily. Stop in at the boutiques, the shops, the bars, the cafes. Have souffles at Cafe Jacqueline, buy a curio at the Schlock Shop. Notice that just off Grant on the cross streets there are bakeries whose wares are fresh right now. Stop in at the galleries, the postcard palace, and Figoni's, one of the last true hardware stores in urban America, and don't miss the evening show at The Old Spaghetti Factory. But when you come to the corner of Grant and Vallejo, pause.

On the southwest corner of the street is the Caffe Trieste, the premier Bohemian coffee house of the area. Founded in

1954, it is a world-famous catalyst of avant-garde culture, and remains a beloved gathering place of writers and artists—as well as of stockbrokers and lawyers taking an early morning coffee on the way to the Financial District. It is said that Francis Ford Coppola edited his manuscript for *The Godfather* while sipping coffee here. On Saturdays, at noon, a popular opera and folk song sing-along here features the Trieste's owners, some good local talent, and, occasionally, a touring diva or two. West on Vallejo, to Columbus, you'll find the Church of St. Francis of Assisi, founded in 1849 as the first Catholic parish church in California after the Missions. It survived the 1906 Quake, which makes it venerable in ways few San Francisco buildings can be.

Continuing north on Vallejo, across Columbus from this church, you'll see Molinari's, the most remarkable of the many remarkable old-world-style delicatessens in North Beach. Continuing farther up Vallejo toward Russian Hill, you'll pass the Postermat across Stockton Street, and my favorite habitué, the Caffe Italia. If, however, you're here in pleasant weather, a picnic lunch from Molinari's, eaten in Washington Square Park, followed by a cappucino at Trieste, is almost enough to make you an honorary Italian-American. Turning right onto Columbus you'll be passing many more cafes, shops, and sights. The fresco-like murals of Caffe Roma are worth the visit. Short of listing each one, I can only suggest you keep your eyes open and stop wherever you like. At the five-pointed intersection ahead of you, looking west on Columbus toward Fisherman's Wharf, the important cross-street is Green. To your left across Columbus on Green, nearly a full block away, is the Fugazi Building, which currently houses one of San Francisco's longest-running, most entertaining theatrical demonstrations, *Beach Blanket Babylon,* in a cabaret-style theatre. There are numerous restaurants and bars in the area, as well as the Italian-American Museum that promotes Italian-American art, history, and culture. To your right at the intersection, popular bars and restaurants lead you back to Grant, most notable being the Caffe Sport (seafood) and the New Pisa (family-style restaurant).

As I said, North Beach is my favorite part of this, my favorite town. I could happily stop with you in virtually every shop and cafe along these streets. But you know your own time best. Go where you will, as far as your peripatetic bon vivant tendencies will allow, and see if North Beach's allure will enchant you, as it has so many millions of people before. And when you're ready, we'll move on to a very different part of The City.

In no part of San Francisco is it as difficult as it is in North Beach to suggest places to go, things to do, or bars and restaurants to eat and relax in. This is not because there are no good spots, but because there are so many; the area deserves a book of listings all its own. We currently have a North Beach book in progress, but until it is finished (1985-1986), I can only single out some of my favorites here. If the list seems unduly long, you can only imagine how many excellent places I've had to leave out. For example, North Beach has many live Jazz clubs, comedy clubs, and places to dance whose locations change with some frequency. If these are your entertainments, become a San Francisco pioneer: go out and find one of your own. My list here is a guide, and should by no means be taken as the last word.

Shops, etc:

Biordi Italian Imports. 412 Columbus Avenue. 392-8096.

A. Cavalli Italian Book Store. 1441 Stockton Street. 421-4219.

City Lights Books. 261 Columbus Avenue. 362-8193.

Figoni Hardware Co. 1318 Grant Avenue. 392-8411.

Molinari Italian Delicatessen. 373 Columbus Avenue. 421-2337.

Museo Italo Americano. 678 Green Street. 398-2660.

North Beach Museum (in the Eureka Federal Savings Building). 1435 Stockton Street. 626-7070.

Poor Taste (collectables and unique miscellany). 1562 Grant Avenue. 982-5539.

Postermat (current and collectable poster art). 401 Columbus Avenue. 421-5536.

Quantity Postcards. 1402 Grant Avenue. 986-8866.

Stella Pastry. 446 Columbus Avenue. 986-2914.

Cafes:

Bohemian Cigar Store. 566 Columbus Avenue. 362-0536.

Caffe Italia. 708 Vallejo Street. 362-9315.

Caffe Puccini. 411 Columbus Avenue. 989-7034.

Caffe Roma. 414 Columbus Avenue. 391-8584.

Caffe Trieste. 609 Vallejo Street. 392-6739.

Enrico's. 504 Broadway. 392-6220. (Sidewalk cafe and restaurant.)

Savoy-Tivoli. 1438 Grant Avenue. 362-7023. (Sidewalk cafe and restaurant.)

Restaurants:

Alfred's. 886 Broadway. 781-7058. **$$

Amelio's. 1630 Powell Street. 397-4339. **$$$

Caffe Grifone. 1609 Powell Street. 397-8458. **$$

Caffe Sport. 574 Green Street. 981-1251. **$½

Dante's. 430 Columbus Avenue. 956-0676. *$½

Des Alpes. 732 Broadway. 391-4249. (Family style dining.)*$

Fior d'Italia. 601 Union Street. 986-1886. **$$$

Greek Taverna. 256 Columbus Avenue. 362-7260. (Night club with belly dancing.) *$$

Guido's. 347 Columbus Avenue. 982-2157. **$$

Julius Castle. On Telegraph Hill. 1541 Montgomery Street. 362-3042. (Marvelous views). **$$

Little Joe's. 523 Broadway. 433-4343. **$

La Mirabelle. 1326 Powell Street. 421-3374. ***$$$

New Pisa. 550 Green Street. 362-4726. (Family style dining.) *$

North Beach Restaurant. 1512 Stockton Street. 392-1587. **$$½

Rick's Cafe American. 317 Columbus Avenue. 981-8266. *$½

Tommaso Famous Pizzeria. 1042 Kearny Street. 398-9696. (Noted for Pizza.) ***$½

Vanessi's. 498 Broadway. 421-0890. **$$

Washington Square Bar & Grill. 1707 Powell Street. 982-8123. **$$

Bars and Public Houses and other entertainment:

Enrico's. 504 Broadway. 392-6220.

Finocchio Club. 506 Broadway. 982-9388. (Female impersonator revues.)

Gino and Carlo (classic S.F. working persons' bar). 548 Green Street. 421-0896.

Little City Antipasti Bar. Union and Powell. 434-2900.

North Star. 1560 Powell Street. 397-0577.

Old Spaghetti Factory (this is the original—a "must" visit). 478 Green Street. 421-0221. *

Savoy-Tivoli. 1438 Grant Avenue. 362-7023.

Spec's. 12 Adler Alley. 421-4112.

Wolfgang's (formerly the Boarding House and the Old Waldorf). 901 Columbus Avenue. 441-4333. (Live entertainment by headline performers.)

Tosca Cafe. 242 Columbus Avenue. 986-9651. (Opera on the jukebox.)

Vesuvio Cafe. 255 Columbus Avenue. 362-3370.

Washington Square Bar & Grill. 1707 Powell. 982-8123.

Andiamo. 723 Vallejo. 362-9402.

(Note: Family-Style dining is a San Francisco institution in North Beach—usually, you share long tables with festive others and pass around the nourishing fixed courses, and the conversation, in "family style." These places will stuff you—five or six hearty courses with wine at an unbelievably cheap price—so go hungry. There are numerous Family-Style restaurants in the North Beach area.)

Maiden Lane
and a Stroll Down Market Street

By catching a Cable Car at Columbus and Mason, or back at Union and Mason, just up from Washington Square, you can ride down from North Beach back to Union Square, and have another opportunity to see anything you may have missed from the Union Square chapter on p. *33*. Moreover, when you're ready to move on, being at Union Square will provide you with a chance to see another unusual piece of The City's history in nearby Maiden Lane. This two-block exploration will bring you to a point near Market Street—the focal point of this chapter's stroll.

*Alas, as this book went to press the Old Spaghetti Factory closed for the last time. Check location as new establishment is planned.

Ideally, your walk starts on the east side of Union Square, across the park from the Cable Car tracks. In the middle of that block you will find the passageway in question. A century ago this little by-way we call Maiden Lane was called Morton Street. It was not, as it is today, known for its quaint or exclusive shops, but for its violence and prostitution. Indeed, this tiny thoroughfare reportedly harbored some of the worst, as well as some of the most popular, whorehouses in all this wild and woolly town. While painted ladies and shady streets were nothing new to The City, Morton Street bordellos were reportedly famous for the "special depravity and variety" of their women.

Part of Morton Street's attraction, in its glory days, was its location in the midst of an otherwise fashionable business community. In 1906, when this red light district burned along with so much else, The City demonstrated its innate (if in this case unwitting) sense of humor in renaming the blocks as it did.

Among Morton Street's most notorious personalities was a madam who went by the handle of Iodoform Kate, after the color of the iodine compound that matched her red hair. According to the legend, competition was so fierce in the alley that it was difficult for a madam to make a living, let alone retire in the splendid wealth Iodoform envisioned. But supposedly Kate was not unread; as a free-lance student in the then-new field of psychology, she was familiar from her studies with the newly-introduced term, *nymphomania*. Now, clinically speaking today, nymphomania is not quite what popular belief holds it to be; and it is plausible that much of our contemporary misunderstanding of the term derives from Iodoform's lust for making money.

Gauging her clientele with a shrewd eye, Iodoform began to advertise that she and all her girls were not only Jewish and red heads (a San Francisco tradition of the time held Jewish women and red heads to be the best lovers), but were also lately come down with the "disease of insatiable sexual appetite" as well. Business boomed. Tourists and sailors from around the world bought Iodoform's scam and spread the word about nymphomania. Soon thereafter, our heroine retired in wealth and comfort.

Ah, well. Red lights and Iodoform are things of the past, as is Morton Street. Maiden Lane now offers other sorts of delights. Tucked away in its brief length you can find designer fashions, fabrics, and jewelry, the renowned Orvis fishing goods outlet, Robinson's Pet Store (one of the nation's oldest), and the well-known Iron Horse drinking establishment. You will also find a fine example of Frank Lloyd Wright's architecture—supposedly the only building he ever designed that is flanked on two sides by other buildings. It is called the Morris Building, and its brick front and round, swirling entryway are unmistakable, just a few doors into the Lane from Union Square, on your left. For years, it housed the internationally famous boutique of Helga Howie, now moved to 60 Maiden Lane. Today, it is an art gallery and as such bears a striking interior resemblance to Wright's Gugenheim Museum in New York.

Amble as you wish down the two-block-long alley to its eastern outlet. Turn right onto Kearny Street and walk one block on to Market Street. Pause. On your left you can see a street island where a rather homely-looking monument stands; this item was, at one time, a lamp with a fountain providing water to horses and pedestrians. This beloved piece of inelegance was built well before the 1906 Earthquake, and has been the scene of many and sundry gatherings, including a now-annual memorial service held at its base each April 18 to commemorate the anniversary of the Great Quake. It is known as Lotta's Fountain, after the lady who had it built as her gift to The City, Lotta Crabtree.

How to explain Lotta? San Francisco has always adored theatre. Indeed, all California has long been a haven for thespians, dramatists, and entertainers of every stamp. The City's theatrical reputation began because the large population that congregated here during the Gold Rush was starved for entertainment, and it quickly became apparent to actors and singers from the East Coast and Europe that such a cultural vacuum could be construed as a new land of opportunity. They were right: not only were they handsomely paid for their efforts, they were also extraordinarily well received and greatly appreciated here.

Lotta Crabtree was one of the most famous dancers and ladies of the stage in the whole of the Victorian era. Raised in a mining camp in the first years of the Gold Rush, she was introduced to dancing at an early age through a chance friendship with the beautiful and notorious Lola Montez,* which included tutoring sessions for young Lotta in dance, singing, and other stage arts. The friendship was brief, but it shaped Lotta Crabtree's destiny as a star.

Lotta was an avant-garde entertainer. She joked, talked, and laughed with her audience, ad-libbed her lines, and generally ignored the formal stage etiquette of the time altogether. Her unusual approach to performing shocked many staid theatregoers when she toured New York, Boston, Philadelphia, London, and the other provinces; but by and large audiences loved her carefree sincerity and her warm, open style at least as much as they loved her considerable talent.

Lotta never married; her life was totally devoted to the stage. When she died, in 1924, she willed much of her nearly $4 million estate to various charities. To San Francisco, the city she loved above all others, she left a world of now-forgotten memories and Lotta's Fountain.

Across Market Street to the south is the construction site of the huge Yerba Buena complex, a massive redevelopment project dominated by the newly completed George Moscone Convention Center. (See Appendix, p. *162* .) Originally, this section of town was referred to as "south of the slot," because of the Cable Car slots that ran down Market Street prior to 1906. At that time, South of the Slot was a residential

---

*Lola Montez was the major spectacle during The City's theatrical seasons in the early 1850s, when her sensational "Spider Dance" took San Francisco by storm. In 1856, following an ill-fated tour of Australia, she was broke; and so, she sold her jewels to Joseph Duncan's jewelry store here. The sale provides one of those remarkable pieces of historic coincidence that makes the least devout among us wonder at the role Fate plays in our lives; for Joseph Duncan was to become the father of San Francisco's most famous dancer of all, Isadora Duncan. But that, as they say, is another story.

neighborhood known as "Happy Valley." After the Quake it turned gradually to light industry. Today, it is a focal point of controversy over high-rise development. However it is becoming increasingly fashionable, and contains a bit of everything—homes, small businesses, large office complexes, a fine variety of restaurants and bars, unusual theatres and art galleries, parks, designer showplaces, and artists' studios. The new, French owned L'hôtel Méridien is, itself, well worth a visit. Located at 50 Third Street at Market (974-6400), this hostelry is the ultimate in what may be described as modern Parisian chic and is The City's newest first-class hotel.

Market Street is one of The City's oldest thoroughfares. Probably—no one seems to be certain—named after Philadelphia's Market Street, it was first laid out between 1845 and 1847 by Jasper O'Farrell, one of San Francisco's first surveyors. Some local citizens were irate with Mr. O'Farrell's proposal for the street because of its unusually wide boundaries. But his vision that Market Street would become The City's primary commercial and dividing boulevard has proved correct.

At the far western end of the street you can see the tips of Twin Peaks, an area named for the two nearly identical 1000-foot-high mountainous hills standing out against the sky. At the eastern end, you can see the clock tower of the Ferry Building, where you catch your boats to Sausalito and points north (see Appendix, p. *159*).

Turn toward the Ferry Building and begin your stroll down Market Street while I tell you some of the extraordinary history of this part of town.

In the 1880s and 1890s, until the Golden Era was brought to its cruel end by the destruction of 1906, this section of the boulevard was known as the "cocktail route." It was the area where gentlemen in Prince Alberts and top hats went after work to take their libations and to enjoy refined or rude conversation in the dozens of elegantly appointed and sumptuously furnished saloons that dotted the route, mostly from Powell (where you boarded your first Cable Car, on p. *26*) to Montgomery Street, just ahead of us now. This strip was world famous in those days. Indeed, the idea and custom of the "free lunch," and even the "cocktail" itself, are said to have originated on this route; and it was routine for patrician men and all the aspiring male optimates to "make the route" in the afternoon, indulging in free food and—if we can believe the reports—five or ten or even twenty or more "cocktails" before wending their tipsy ways home.

The custom of the free lunch as part of a bar's service was a San Francisco institution. While the custom came to be enjoyed in other cities of the day, it reached its zenith right here on this street. Oscar Lewis, in his classic book *Bay Window Bohemia,* offers this as one of many examples:

"That San Francisco's pre-eminence in (this) regard was justly earned becomes clear when one considers the viands daily set forth to tempt the appetites of patrons of a single resort, this one being Charley Newman's Yellowstone Bar on Montgomery Street. For at its counter, which extended the entire length of the long room, and was presided over by a corps of white-clad Chinese waiters, were to be found at all times such delicacies as Camembert, Brie, Gorgonzola, Limburger, and a half a dozen other cheeses, caviar, guava sandwiches, sweetbreads on toast, alligator pear salad with nasturtium leaves, diamond-back terrapin from Maryland, Virginia ham baked in French brandy, roast venison, clams fried in chopped olives and corn meal, shrimps in jellied creme de menthe, and—for those with less exotic tastes—roast beef, pork, lamb, and corned beef with cabbage. Incredible as it sounds in the present Spartan era, when a bowl of pretzels or salted peanuts constitutes about all in the way of provender laid out at our cocktail bars, this bountiful offering was by no means unique. The Yellowstone's menu was, in fact, looked on as strictly run-of-the-mill . . . those elaborate feasts were served to all comers, the man whose only purchase was a five-cent schooner of beer being no less welcome than the most prodigal spenders."

Some of the more popular cocktails of that era were the "Stone Wall" (Jamaican rum and cider), the "Sazarac" (rye whiskey, a dash of bitters, and absinthe shaken with ice and served in a glass well-rubbed with anisette, and which was made famous by San Francisco's lovely southern sister in good living, New Orleans), and the "Black Velvet" (champagne with a float of stout). The prodigious self-indulgence of the free lunch and the cocktail route amazes most people today, but during San Francisco's Champagne Age, such lusty crapulence was apparently the way of life. And, according to the records, all this eating and drinking that took place near where we are walking now was, as often as not, but an *hors d'oeuvre* to a late evening supper—at least for those whose bellies and purses were still capable.

The only extant example of an old Cocktail Route establishment is the popular Hoffman's Grill, located on Market Street just past the Palace Hotel, east of New Montgomery. Its spread is neither so bountiful nor so cheap as what Charley Newman offered, but its decor is largely unchanged these many years, and the lunchtime crowds still belly up enthusiastically for the hearty food and drink. (As of this writing, a new highrise is planned to occupy the block; but Hoffman's plans to be incorporated, virtually unchanged, into the new building.)

The tradition and love of eating and drinking—albeit somewhat tempered—is still a salient feature of The City's lifestyle today. Statistics readily demonstrate that San Francisco is the eatingest and drinkingest city in America. It has been claimed by some reliable reports that there are currently close to five thousand bars and restaurants operating in The City's scant seven-mile-square area, serving a resident population of seven-hundred-thousand people. Of course, the per capita alcoholism rate is also higher in San Francisco than anywhere else in America, but perhaps we can write off this unfortunate footnote to tradition, or to the fog. Either way, it is not a statistic to be proud of.

The watering holes from which the fabulous free lunches and exotic drinks spewed forth were not content merely with stuffing their patrons full of food and paralyzing them with booze. Their decor was frequently overdone as well, displaying a vulgar, gaudy opulence that was, despite itself, both charming and comfortable, in a quintessential Victorian fashion. Bas-relief ceilings of satyrs and nymphs, marble floors, mahogany and rosewood bars, cut crystal and art glass, brass trimmings, gas lamps, and other expensive bric-a-brac were the order of the day. And one item was obligatory in every Gay Nineties San Francisco bar: art.

Depending on the bar and its location, some one or more of its walls would be graced by paintings that were ordinarily unremarkable, often executed by local artists, and hung in gilded frames. These paintings ranged across the whole gamut of Romantic Kitsch. But for the urbane clientele of the cocktail route, "art" consisted almost exclusively of wanton and remarkably abundant female nudes, which—or who—were depicted in all manner of poses against a wide variety of stylized landscapes. The overarching themes were Biblical or historical, no doubt to morally justify the vast expanses of skin. But regardless of theme, the female subjects were invariably buxom, corpulent, and scantily clad. The establishment most famous for displaying this genre of work was happily called The Palace of Art. All its walls were covered with naked ladies in gilded frames, hung as closely together as space would allow.

Perhaps reflecting the prurient titillation inside the bars of the cocktail route, each evening The City's loveliest *nymphs du pave* began their nightly promenade along the streets that intersected Market; and here, also, some of the era's most fashionable *maisons de joie* opened their doors to business. But on at least one other Market Street corner, a different kind of business was in progress; and you need not walk much further down the street before arriving at the site: one of San Francisco's greatest landmarks and one of the world's great hotels, the Palace. Located between New Montgomery and Third Streets on the south side of Market and Montgomery, and now owned by the Sheraton hotel chain, the Palace was the first truly large, *grand luxe* hotel in America.

The first Palace—this is the second; the first one burned

in 1906—was built by William Ralston and opened its doors in October, 1875. The boastful claim that it was "the world's grandest hotel" was not much of an exaggeration. Ralston's partners thought him a bit daft for wanting to erect such a colossal resort, but he sank no less than five million 1870s dollars—almost exactly the sum spent in the same era to build New York's Central Park—into what became an instant legend and the talk of world travellers everywhere.

Statistics alone cannot really convey the scale of Ralston's toy, as it was known in his day, but more than a century ago a structure of such size, sporting such features and opulence, merely dumbfounded most people.

The hotel was seven stories high and almost a quarter-mile in circumference. It had more than 800 rooms and two basements, a huge central Grand Court atrium surrounded by seven grand galleries and surmounted by a dome of translucent glass. Its grand entrance was, and it is today, from New Montgomery Street, and was designed so that the carriages of arriving guests might drive directly into the building. Nearly every room was equipped with such modern amenities as wash basins, flush toilets, bathtubs, and fireplaces. The ceilings in most rooms exceeded fifteen feet in height. Five hydraulic elevators finished with brass and mirror-faced walls and lounge seats carried guests up and down. Telephones and electric lights were installed soon after the hotel opened, and from the beginning its fittings and furnishings would have delighted any Roman emperor or French Louis. They included nine hundred gold-plated cuspidors standing on such an array of the best carpet available that W. & J. Sloane came to San Francisco from New York to establish a branch office, and stayed for more than one hundred years.

Needless to say, the Palace's show of extravagant luxury impressed the worldliest visitor. Equally so, in those days, did the quality of the hotel's service, and the gastronomic extravagances of its chefs and kitchens. The following menu was served at the Palace banquet honoring Senator William Sharon, one of the Comstock Lode millionaires and Ralston's business partner, on 8 February 1876.

Huitres
Chablis
Consommé Royal
Sherry Isabella
Saumon Glacé au four à la Chambord
Sauterne
Boudin blanc à la Richelieu
Château la Tour
Filet de Boeuf à la Providence
Champagne
Pâté de Fois Gras
Château d'Yquem
Timbale de Volaille Américaine au Senateur
Clos Vougeot
Cotelettes d'Agneau sauté au pointes d'Asperges
Sorbet
Becassine au Cresson
Château Margeaux
Salade à la Francaise
Déssert

The bill of fare was engraved on a sheet of solid silver for each of the several dozen guests to keep as a memento of the occasion.

The list of notable, noble, famous, and simply wealthy magnificoes who have enjoyed the hotel's supreme luxury reads like a century-long *Who's Who* of governors, royalty, dignitaries, and entertainers. Much of its history complements that of the man who built it.

The flamboyant, melodramatic William C. Ralston was a former Mississippi River boatman who arrived in San Francisco with the Gold Rush. In the mid-1860s, with several partners, he organized the Bank of California, which quickly established itself as the leading financial institution in the West—a position it enjoyed for many years. The big, affable Ralston had his office in the Bank's headquarters at California and Sansome Streets, a location it occupies to this day, and he reportedly would circulate among his customers with jovial flourishes while his tellers and cashiers, surrounded by huge stacks of gold, dispatched business from a low mahogany table in the center of the room, with no cages separating them from the patrons.

Ralston's Lucullian style became world famous. Besides his modest townhouse mansion just off the top of Nob Hill, he constructed a veritable palace as his country home in the suburb of Belmont, some 20 miles south of The City. The estate's private stables and gas plant alone cost more than one-hundred-thousand 1870s dollars. It still exists today as a convent well cared for by nuns, and it can be visited.

Belmont became *de rigeur* for all the famous people who visited California in those days. Ralston reportedly decided to best his eastern counterparts' yachts by having special luxury trains transport his guests from extravagant parties held in the townhouse to even more extravagant ones held simultaneously at Belmont. The trains then carried the guests back to the townhouse party in a round-robin of drinking and merry-making which sometimes lasted for days.

Ralston's grand style was not restricted to lavish entertainments. In 1869, when the aftermath of the Civil War and California's riches had helped inflate the national economy enough to cause a nation wide depression, the government in Washington temporarily suspended the minting of gold coin, as well as the exchange of currency for gold bullion. One result of this action was that the United States Mint in San Francisco was temporarily closed, and the local banks, with their tons of gold bullion, were functionally broke. Some suspect that the East Coast plutocrats were behind this as a scheme to break the rising wealth and power of the West Coast.

A rumor that the San Francisco banks could not meet the demands of their depositors, and the run on the banks such a rumor would engender, would have spelled disaster for The City and for California industry in general. Ralston is said to have laughed at the irony of his and other banks' vaults bulging with gold which was prohibited in the marketplace, but he did not find the situation funny. Clearly, he needed several million dollars in gold coin, and he needed it fast.

Market Street, c.1880's, looking north up Kearny Street from 3rd Street. Note Lotta's Fountain.

The United States Subtreasury in San Francisco had the coin, but President Grant's order placed it effectively out of reach. So, according to the story, Ralston robbed the United States Subtreasury!

Actually, he did not quite *rob* the Subtreasury. Rather, he *exchanged* an equal amount of his temporarily worthless gold bullion for each coin he removed from the vaults. No one was the loser and, for a time at least, no one was the wiser. How Ralston accomplished his unprecedented feat remains a mystery to this day. But he was loved and trusted by almost everyone of importance in The City. If some bank guard or guards looked the other way, and if they were well rewarded for doing so, their action must have been regarded as more a matter of civic duty than of greed. Certainly for the men involved, the greater honor lay in saving San Francisco than in obeying the rules disdainful foreigners in Washington laid down.

In any case, neither legal retribution nor scandal devolved from Ralston's wonderfully outrageous scheme. When the predictable run on the banks did occur, Ralston reportedly greeted his anxious patrons with a gracious smile, surrounded by stacks of gold coin two and three feet high.

Not all was idyllic in Ralston's life however. Flamboyant and popular a benefactor of The City as he was, he did not live to see his magnificent dream completed. Other economic crises struck during the hotel's construction, and Ralston and his bank soon found themselves severely overextended. In time, both went into receivership. The bank reorganized and continued on as a sound and respected financial institution; but the passing flap apparently taxed Ralston beyond his ability to cope, and he drowned while taking one of his customary swims in the Bay two months before the Palace first opened its doors.

As I noted a few pages back, the Sheraton-Palace that stands now is the second one. The first Palace was not seriously damaged by the Earthquake itself, but the resulting holocaust that was to reduce four-fifths of the downtown area to ashes, was also to claim the Palace. Like the rest of San Francisco, a new Palace rose from the ruins of the old, and the present hotel opened its door to the new era in 1909.

The most striking feature of the new Palace is its huge, elegant, art-glass-domed atrium dining room, the Garden Court. This spectacular room is famous for its lavish Sunday brunch, and for the presence of the San Francisco String Quartet, which often plays at dinner. It is claimed as the most elegant dining room in America, and few will argue the point. Among the hotel's other bars and restaurants, the Pied Piper is particularly worth a stop for the original Maxfield Parrish painting which hangs over the bar, and after which it is named.

As you stand outside the hotel facing east on Market Street, the Financial District of San Francisco is on your left, north across the street up Montgomery; we shall discuss that part of town shortly. Ahead of you, east down Market, is the Ferry Buiding and the World Trade Center. It is about five blocks down Market Street to the California Street Cable Car line, whose eastern terminus is outside the Hyatt Regency Hotel near the Ferry Building, at the intersections of California, Market, and Drumm. This is where we shall pick up our tour again at the start of the following chapter.

Partly because Market Street, including the Financial District, has undergone a radical transformation since the 1960s, and partly because it is an area increasingly devoted to new towering and inartistic office structures, I do not offer my usual list of suggestions at the conclusion of this chapter. However, I do suggest you walk down this grand boulevard as with each new highrise complex, there will be new shops, restaurants, saloons and sights.

Note: There are plans to utilize the old streetcar tracks on Market (surface trolleys on Market were recently replaced by the MUNI'S METRO underground tram system), and combine them with other tracks along The Embarcadero into a new streetcar system that will run down Market from Civic Center, around past the Ferry Building, through the Fisherman's Wharf complex to the Fort Mason cultural area. What will be fun and unusual about this system—if it happens—is that the plans call for only antique streetcars to be used; and, in fact, a collection of early twentieth century "Iron Monsters" from around the world is being assembled and tested for this purpose as I write this. Current plans are to make the 1983 Festival an annual summer event. The idea is a grand one that makes a lot of sense, and if and when this proposed new trolley line of old trams does become full-fledged reality, it will add another delightfully unique aspect to your tour . . . and another chapter to this book.

THE CALIFORNIA STREET LINE
California and Market

I f you have been observant, you may have noticed that the Cable Cars on this line look different from those on the Powell Street lines, in that they are double-ended cars having grips at both ends. This difference reflects the fact that the California Cars are not spun around on turntables when they have to change directions, as the Powell Cables are. They run in both directions instead, using a crossover

track to change direction. The Gripman and Conductor simply switch ends.*

---

*During the rebuilding of the Cable Cars, plans called for all of the Powell lines turntables to be enlarged to accomodate the larger California Cars, should this be desired or needed in the future to accommodate tentative plans to augment the system's versatility by running some California Cars over Hyde to Ghirardelli Square, in effect creating a new line. Ironically, until the early 1950s, it was the California Street Cars that operated on Hyde (the Powell Cars then running out through Pacific Heights along Washington and Jackson Streets); so our proposed new line—if it happens—is really the partial reestablishment of more San Francisco tradition.

Contemporary view of a California Street Cable Car in the Financial District. Photo was taken just prior to the 1982 shutdown for restoration. Note the "Save The Cable Cars Telethon" ad.

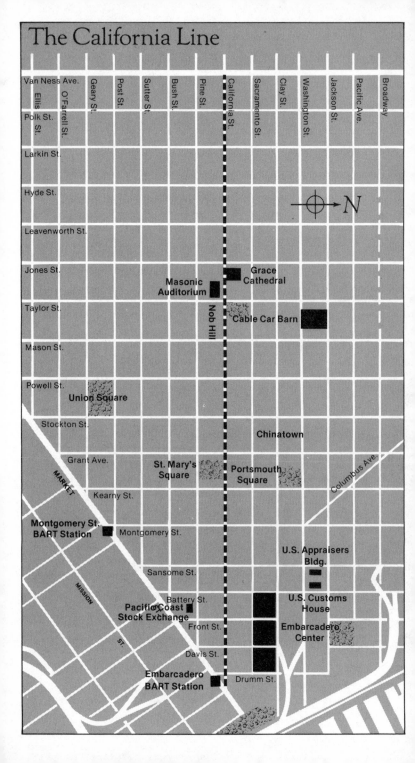

This line was built originally in 1878 by former Governor, later Senator, Leland Stanford, it is said, so that his wife, Mrs. Jane Lathrop Stanford, could shop without having to climb the Nob Hill steps afterwards, coming home. Now it begins at Robert Frost Plaza at California and Market Streets (the poet, Frost, was a native son), rolls up California Street through the Financial District, rises over Nob Hill, and slides down a decline locals regard as gentle to its western end between Polk Street and Van Ness Avenue.

While many of the sights along the California line are best explored when you are on your own, there are four areas in particular I would like to call to your attention in the chapters to come: the Embarcadero Center/Maritime Plaza; the once-infamous Barbary Coast, now fashionable Jackson Square; the Financial District, often referred to as Wall Street West; and Nob—sometimes ingallantly called Snob—Hill. These four parts of town may constitute the most diverse symbiosis The City offers in a small geographic area. They represent the old and the new, the rich and the poor, the best and the worst San Francisco has ever seen. Nob Hill, named for the wealth that rose to its heights like cream to the top of The City's golden milk bottle; the Barbary Coast, named for the dregs of humanity that accumulated there like silt; the Financial District, representing one of the greatest concentrations of wealth in the world; and the monolithic towers of the Embarcadero Center, a redeveloped urban area that is practically a city within itself. Finally, at the western end of the California line, there is another part of town worth your time if you are somewhat adventuresome: the quaint and colorful Polk Street. (Note: the California line passes Grant Avenue/Chinatown as it climbs to the top of Nob Hill from the Financial District.)

Above you will find a map embracing all five sections; each is reviewed in turn as it appears there.

Embarcadero Center

Regarded from the northeast, the spectacular and glamorous Hyatt Regency Hotel does resemble, as one wag noted, a

typewriter lying on its side. But from the inside, with its magnificent seventeen-story atrium lobby, fountains, hanging gardens, and light-and-glass-bell-shaped exposed elevators, it becomes a vast cathedral of the future. Part of Hyatt's world-wide chain of first-class hostelries, the Regency, where even Princes have been known to gawk, demands a visit. You can wander around at the atrium level (third floor above the street) until you're lost, or sit in one of the bars or restaurants there, or ride to the revolving Equinox bar high above the madding crowd to enjoy an everchanging panorama of The City and the Bay.

Down on the street, at the Robert Frost Plaza's Market Street side, and to the east, in the huge plaza behind the hotel dominated by the Vallencourt Fountain, entertainments are appropriately more pedestrian. Here, street artists, musicians, and public entertainers of various sorts strut their stuff on a regular basis. They are a pleasing sidelight if you are in

Nob Hill today. View at Mason & California Streets showing Grace Cathedral & the Pacific Union Club.

the area, or if you are walking down Market toward the Ferry Building.

The Ferry Building, which is scheduled for major restoration soon, is identifiable by its grand clock tower. The building was erected in the decade before our famous Earthquake. Until the 1930s, when the San Francisco-Oakland Bay Bridge and the Golden Gate Bridge were built, when ferries were the only way to get to and from the different cities around the Bay, it was among the busiest ferry terminals in the world. In those days a great fleet of huge ferry boats plied these waters hauling many thousands of commuters each hour. When the bridges opened, the commuters could drive from place to place, the ferry services were discontinued and the big boats became fond memories. But change is nothing if not constant: in 1970, a few new ferries began to serve the Bay as an experiment in alternative transportation. At present, they serve Sausalito, Tiburon, and Larkspur Landing from the same old Ferry Building. If you decide on a ferry ride as part of your San Francisco visit, be sure to verify fares and schedules in advance (see Appendix, p. *159* , for information). The Ferry Building, which presently incorporates our World Trade Center, is also headquarters for the Port of San Francisco and other offices.

As a port, San Francisco is far less used today than it was in the past. Most modern shipping is container cargo, which demands large flat land facilities far more readily available at the world's fifth-largest port, the Port of Oakland, farther into the Bay. Shipping still comes through The City, of course, but for the most part its piers are now devoted to navy and cruise ships. Some heavy shipping and huge dry docks are still in place, far south from the Ferry Building, but it is not an area to walk to.

Speaking of transportation, it is impossible to miss the freeway that partly obscures the grandeur of the old Ferry Building; and you can see that one branch of the roadway ends abruptly, going nowhere. In the late 1950s and early 1960s, The City's population rebelled against what has awkwardly been called the "Los Angelization" of San Francisco, and raised a loud hue and cry against lengthening the miles of local freeways. When the issue came to a head, the citizenry here passed the first and only law in the United States banning further freeway construction, and stopping the progress of this one on the spot. As of this writing, a proposal sits before our city government to demolish this unique eyesore as part of the waterfront's general restoration.

Across the Embarcadero roadway just to the south from the Ferry Building, under the freeway at the foot of Mission Street, stands the lovely Audiffred Building. Erected in 1889 by a Parisian expatriate, Hippolite d'Audiffred, who is said to have walked the 3,000 miles from Veracruz, Mexico, to San Francisco in escaping the anti-Maximillian revolt, it reflects the French mansard style typical of old buildings along Paris' Champs Elysee. Originally a warehouse, the Audiffred Building later became the first headquarters of the world's first seaman's union, which evolved into the Sailors Union of the Pacific, and the International Seaman's Union.

Audiffred made a fortune selling charcoal to the Chinese, who needed it as fuel to run their laundries and boilers, and when the flames of 1906 threatened the building, he bribed firemen to save it by securing bottles of whiskey and wine from the bartender of his tenant, the Bulkhead Saloon. When the Saloon closed a few years later, the Bank of America opened one of its early branches in its space. The great Waterfront Strike of 1934 began in this building; Harry Bridges, the president of the International Longshoremen's Union, had his offices in the Building for years; and to this day marine union members gather at or near the Audiffred every 5th of July to remember Bloody Thursday. After World War II the Building was owned by Wayne Collins, who achieved fame as Tokyo Rose's lawyer. In recent years the Audiffred Building housed the Riordan Saloon, one of The City's famous two-fisted drinking joints. Although the Audiffred survived the 1906 devastation, fire gutted the building in 1978; but when the wrecking ball seemed inevitable, a public-spirited businessman from Australia, Dusan Mills, spent millions to restore the structure to its former glory, as you see it today. It houses a good saloon, too.

Embarcadero Center itself is made up principally of four similar tower buildings with interconnecting, open-space lower levels. It advertises itself as "The City Side of San Francisco," and with its hundreds of businesses at street and mezzanine levels, and thousands of offices above, it is largely what it claims to be, in the tradition of New York's Rockefeller Plaza which is said to have inspired it.

For many generations, the blocks the complex occupies were San Francisco's produce district. The colorful display of wholesale farm products, warehouses and salty workers has now moved to the south side of town. Instead, the Embarcadero buildings are flanked by the Maritime Plaza and the Golden Gateway Center to the north, offering pleasant walkways and open green belts in which employees of local firms take lunch, and in which you, too, are welcome to relax. The

shops, restaurants, and galleries here below offer a refreshing diversion from business life above.

In the center of each building's street level there is an illuminated cylindrical sign post. These kiosk-like directories indicate the shops and services available in that quarter of the complex.

From the Hyatt Regency, Robert Frost Plaza, or the start of the California Street Cable Car line, you are closest to Embarcadero Four; the Center's other sections—Three, Two, and One—stand in a westerly progression. Once you have toured all the quarters to your satisfaction, a bridge that leads from the third level of the Embarcadero will carry you to the Maritime Plaza. At the center of this complex stands a large, brown building that is the headquarters for Alcoa Aluminum. Its curious design reflects the local need to make large structures "earthquake-proof." In the case of the Alcoa

North Beach, c. 1880's. This view is east from Russian Hill.

Building, the heavy extra bracing has been exteriorized as part of the design.

Across from the Alcoa Building, is a park-like square, affording some dramatic views. The walkway to the north, leading away from the Embarcadero Center, crosses Washington Street and leads to the third component in this complex of complexes that constitute a large, increasingly important feature of San Francisco's redeveloping waterfront. This is the Golden Gateway Center.

Golden Gateway is the residential arm of San Francisco's new urban center, composed of apartments, townhouses, and condominiums, supported by groceries, drugstores, a movie theatre, and several fine restaurants. North across the Jackson Street overpass lies a small park known as Walton

Square. Ahead, you will be able to see Coit Tower and Telegraph Hill on your left as you cross the footbridge. When you've finished with your wanderings, either return to the Cable Cars through Embarcadero Center, or begin your tour of some of yesteryear's most thrilling days right from here, as we move on to the Old Barbary Coast Area.

The four towers that comprise the Embarcadero Center contain some 150 shops and galleries, in addition to the thousands of offices upstairs. Rather than direct you to any particular stores, I reiterate that each of the towers has its own kiosk-like directories at street level, on which you will find the location of the particular type of shop you may be searching for, whether that is a leather boutique, children's wear, books, or a drug store. I will mention that the Center contains several eateries of note, including:

The Golden Eagle (Embarcadero 4). 982-8831. **$$

Enzo's Ristorante (Embarcadero 3). 981-5530. *$½

Sprout's Coffee Shop (Embarcadero 3). 434-3343. (Health food lunches.) *$

Vanity Fair (Embarcadero 2). 362-3247. (Mexican.)

Shapiro's Drug Store and Soda Fountain (Embarcadero 2). 982-6813.

Scott's Seafood Grill (Embarcadero 3). 433-7444. **$$

And in Maritime Plaza at 444 Battery, The Punch Line Rush Hour Bar and Comedy Night Club offers stand-up comedians in the evenings. 474-3801.

The Old Barbary Coast Area
(Jackson Square)

"(The Barbary Coast) owing almost entirely to the influx of gold seekers and the horde of gamblers, thieves, harlots, politicians and other felonious parasites who battered upon them, there arose a unique criminal district that for almost seventy years was the scene of more viciousness and depravity, but which at the same time possessed more glamor, than

any other area of vice and iniquity on the American
continent."—Herbert Asbury

What more do you need to know? The Barbary Coast
proper was located just west of what is now the Walton
Square Park area, mostly along Pacific and Jackson Streets. It
is the oldest section of the "original" city still standing. The
merging of past and present encourage you to use my lead
and to become your own tour guide here, simply because so
much that was, still is—if in a somewhat different form.

A footnote to a good portion of this book, but to none so
greatly as to this chapter, concerns prostitution and its
attendant pleasures or pains. There may be readers who think
I have dwelt too greatly on this facet of San Francisco's
colorful past. The reason I have spent as much attention on
these activities as I have is that they dominated The City's
earlier days to a degree that is not exactly comprehensible
today. There is an old jingle in San Francisco that goes,

> The miners came in forty-nine,
> The whores in fifty-one,
> And when they got together
> They produced the native son.

Where they got together was the bordellos that ran wide
open all over town, and nowhere to such a great extent as in
the Barbary Coast.

Back in Gold Rush times the ratio of men to women in
The City was something like 25 to 1, and few of the women
were "respectable." Demands were too great, and earnings
too high, for the world's oldest profession not to experience a
spectacular popularity. Several thousand prostitutes arrived
here in those years to work in more than 200 brothels, and
still there weren't enough to satify the region's needs. When
this shortage was coupled with the massive influx of capital
provided by the gold and silver fields, business speculation,
and the like, The City's ladies of the night acquired an
elevated status unique in American history. It was entirely
acceptable in those days for a proper gentleman to arrive at
even the most respectable social function with his Cyprian
lady. The most successful madams owned homes said to be
far better furnished than those of anyone else in town except

the greatest robber barons. While prostitutes in most parts of the world endeavored to appear respectable by imitating the manner and dress of fashionable women, in San Francisco during the Golden Age it was the proper women who often aped the whores; for our ladies of the evening could afford the best fashions from Paris.

Had the Barbary Coast simply been another whorehouse ghetto it probably would have raised few eyebrows. But the gambling houses, saloons, opium dens, and other gross dives of the neighborhood played host to hordes of gangsters, villains, and ne'er-do-wells to a degree than even this frontier town at the edge of the world could not tolerate. In fact, this book would have to have a triple X rating to allow any graphic description of the Coast's perversions.

In its early years the Barbary Coast was known as Sydney Town after the gangs of former and escaped convicts from the British penal colony that Australia was then. The "Sydney Ducks" was the most notorious of the rival gangs of thugs that haunted the Coast, and who are given credit for burning the fledgling city down three or four times in the early 1850s merely to distract the population from their murdering, robbing, and pillaging. The word "hoodlum" came into the language to describe them. It was coined from their accented way of saying "huddle'em" when they would surround a victim.

The shows of the 1890's Barbary Coast would seem quaint today.

Much of the Coast's worst violence ended when the local citizenry formed a Committee of Vigilance in 1851 and hanged several gang leaders in a celebrated ceremony in front of City Hall, then located at Portsmouth Square. After a few more, similar, vigilante actions the Barbary Coast settled down to a quiet life of wanton vice. Indeed, it became chic for society swells to go "slumming" in the Coast's internationally known dance halls in the 1890s.

As the quotation at the beginning of this chapter suggests, the vice ran freely, especially in the 1850s and 60s. In the waterfront dives, whose alleys had such explicative names as Murder Point and Dead Man's Alley, the practice of "shanghaiing" was raised to the level of high art. In fact, the first use of "shanghai" as a verb—to be kidnapped into forced labor—came from the Coast. This nefarious custom, widely practiced at the time, was the method by which unscrupulous sea captains secured new sailing crews after their original crews jumped ship in favor of the gold fields. An intended victim was enticed by a bar waitress to buy a few drinks, one of which was drugged liquor known as a "mickey."

After he passed out the man was sold and loaded aboard a departing ship. When he awakened, hours later, he found himself part of a slave crew. Often, these ships were bound for Shanghai from San Francisco, hence the term. Very often, shanghaied victims were never heard from again.

Attempts to police the Coast in the normal fashion were not especially successful, although, as Herbert Asbury points out:

> "Every policeman assigned to waterfront duty was specially chosen for strength, bravery, and huskiness. He was equipped with the regulation nightstick and pistol and also carried, in a large outside breast pocket within easy reach of his hand, a huge knife a foot or more in length. This fearsom weapon was . . . effective at close quarters . . . (In) several battles beleaguered policemen chopped off the hands of their assailants . . . and (in) at least one . . . the attacking hoodlum was decapitated."

It is a minor and amusing postscript to the Coast's debauched history that while evangelists of every stamp raved that the Earthquake and Fire of 1906 were the result of God's wrath over The City's wicked ways, a large portion of the Barbary Coast survived the conflagration, while numerous holier meccas crumbled and were consumed. The buildings in the Coast that withstood the flames today make up what is now called JACKSON SQUARE, an official historical district and the subject of your modern walk.

Before you begin your tour of the Barbary Coast/Jackson Square region, please refer to the map on p. *112*, where you can see the route I recommend. Remember that you are your own best guide in these blocks, and see as much or as little as you like. Leave Sidney Walton Square Park by walking west up Jackson Street to Battery. The United States Customs House stands on this block to your left, and while it is not really part of the Old Coast Area, you ought to step inside. Its marble stairways and grand design are not to be seen in modern architecture.

Turn right, toward Coit Tower, and head up Battery a half-block to One Jackson Place. Turn left and stroll through the shops and narrow walkway; come out onto Sansome Street, turn right, and walk to Pacific Street. The two blocks up Pacific from here take you through the heart of Jackson

Square. While it would be romantic to aver that all the old buildings here were dens of vivid iniquity, the fact is that a large percentage of them that predate the Earthquake were originally built for more normal commercial purposes. Many of the buildings you are passing that are more than a century old have foundations that rest on the hulls of old windjammers, and serve today as the posh salons for world-famous interior decorators, swank legal firms, exclusive galleries, specialty shops, and a few fine restaurants. The valuable, curious facade that graces 555 Pacific once opened onto the Hippodrome, a famous melodeon theatre. The facade, once thought lewd (indeed, the City Fathers forced the ribbon covering the original nude figures, judging the satyrs to be a bit too "excited"), is by the famous artist Arthur Putnam. During the 1940s a nightclub-restaurant strip called the International Settlement flourished along Pacific. At the corner of Columbus and Pacific, across all the streets that come together here, the impressively colored, pre-earthquake Victorian "skyscraper" is the Columbus Towers Building. Presently, it is owned by movie director Francis Ford Coppola.

Turn down Columbus toward the Pyramid, which is Transamerica Corporation's 853-foot-tall world headquarters, completed in 1972. Some critics have claimed that it was Transamerica's intention to create an unmistakable identity symbol while developing its office space. Transamerica's Board Chairman John Beckett says it was not. But in either case, the Pyramid became an instant San Francisco landmark. *Time* magazine called it "Trans-Egypt," but aesthetics apart—everyone has an opinion about the building's design—the Pyramid stirred much angry controversy during its planning and building because it replaced the majestic old Montgomery Block that had stood on the site since 1853, and was an extraordinarily valuable piece of The City's history. Its loss was unconscionable.

The Montgomery Block, later known affectionately as the "Monkey Block," was San Francisco's first large, reinforced, fire-proof building. It was a prestige address for the first few decades of its existence until, in the 1880s, the lawyers and brokers who had occupied it began to move farther "up-town." Into the space their partings made moved writers, musicians, poets, and artists whose aggregation effected one of the most brilliant, beloved artists' colonies The City (and the world) has ever seen. Residents and guests included Mark Twain, Robert Aitken, Gelett Burgess, Ambrose Bierce, George Sterling, Rudyard Kipling, Porter Garnett, Jack London, Perry Newberry, and Robert Louis Stevenson, as well as Dr. Sun Yat Sen, father of the Republic of China. And, one of the nineteenth century's most famous Bohemian resorts, Duncan Nicol's "Bank Exchange" saloon, hosted the town's most illustrious *boulevardiers* and *viveurs* from here with his renowned Pisco Punch. The Golden Era's most celebrated Bohemian restaurant, Papa Coppa's, with its historic black cat murals, operated next door as the favored area hang out for artists and gourmets alike . . . alas, gone are even the memories of this era.

Turn again into Jackson Street, walk the short block to Montgomery, and go left. Across the street, about 30 yards from the corner, just down from the famous Ernie's Restaurant, is a quaint alley called Gold Street, where we are headed.

Walking down Gold Street, use your imagination to be transported back 100 years to the seedy, seamy days of the Barbary Coast. But, of course, a century ago people like you and me would be unlikely visitors to these streets. As you walk, you'll pass the Assay Office, now an eating house of note; then turn right at Balance Alley in front of 40 Gold Street, and continue back to Jackson. As on this area's other streets you will pass furnishings and art worthy of any mansion tempting the wealthy from the local windows. Turn right onto Jackson and continue about a quarter-block, and you will reach a street called Hotaling Alley. Turn left, and as you follow Hotaling one block back to Washington Street, ruminate on the origins of this street's name.

A.P. Hotaling was a liquor wholesaler whose warehouses here on Jackson Street were spared the ravages of the 1906 disaster, and with them his booze. Thus, by the grace of whatever gods smile on imbibers, was San Francisco visited by yet another corny but beloved quatrain,

If, as some say, God spanked the town
For being over frisky,
Why did He burn the churches down
And save Hotaling's whiskey?

Turn right on Washington and proceed west another quarter block to the intersection of Columbus, Washington, and Montgomery, at the base of the Pyramid. Along the way, you'll see Clown Alley—elegant hamburgers. From here you can conclude your tour of the Barbary Coast with a brief side-trip one-half block up Montgomery back toward Pacific. On the corner to your left as you face west on Montgomery stands the original Transamerica Corporation Building, restored to its splendid Victorian design. It was on this corner, too, that the mighty Bank of America began as the Bank of Italy. In fact, B of A originally owned Transamerica, until the Federal courts separated them in an antitrust suit. Continue up Montgomery past Doro's, another fine example of local gastronomic pleasure, and peer at the beautifully restored Belli Building at 722-4 Montgomery, owned by and named for the flamboyant attorney, Melvin Belli, whose offices are within. If the gate entrance is open, you can walk discreetly back to view the lovely courtyard preserved with judicious attention to the delights of this old structure. On the street nearby you may also note a variety of plaques commemorating such places and events as the first Masonic Lodge and the first Jewish religious service to take place in The City.

Now, reverse your steps and return to the Pyramid at the junction of Montgomery, Washington, and Columbus. From this point you begin your tour of the Financial District. If you'd rather call it a day instead, you can catch the California Cable Car either to Nob Hill or back to the Hyatt Regency (really just a short walk away) by continuing down Montgomery south three more blocks to California Street. All the Cable lines cross atop Nob Hill, so you can transfer to any other line there if you wish. Also, North Beach and Chinatown are each only a few minutes walk from the Pyramid.

As you know by the time you've reached this page, my section on the Barbary Coast is truly a walking tour. The basic sights to see in this section of The City are those you have just seen. However, now that the thugs and the Sydney Ducks are long gone, you can find a number of fine restaurants in the area. Here are my favorites.

Assay Office Bar & Grill. 56 Gold Street. 397-4653. **$$
Bali's. 310 Pacific Street. 982-5059. (This is *the* gathering spot for ballet stars and their fans in San Francisco.) **$$
Ciao. 230 Jackson Street. 982-9500. **$$
Doro's. 714 Montgomery Street. 397-6822. ***$$$
Ernie's. 847 Montgomery Street. 397-5969. **$$$
Jovanello's. 840 Sansome Street. 986-8050. **$$$
MacArthur Park. 607 Front Street. 398-5700. (This becomes a singles bar Friday after 5:00 p.m.) *$$
The Albatross Saloon and Restaurant. 155 Columbus at Pacific. 434-3344. (A classic and historic saloon and a San Francisco tradition.) *$

The Financial District

It is hard to miss the modern side of life here, in the towering, but mostly uninspiring, cathedrals of capitalism that house financial institutions of every kind, including banks representing almost every nation with which America trades. History pervades this area as well, but it is more difficult to see than in the Old Barbary Coast Area. The map on p. *112* highlights a number of the most important sites, and you might use it as a focus for any wider tour you wish to make of these several urban acres.

For the purposes of this book, I assume you are walking over from the Barbary Coast/Jackson Square; from elsewhere in The City, the California Street Cable Car line will bring you within a few blocks of where this chapter opens. Disembark at Montgomery Street and walk north to join us at the corner of Washington Street. If you are continuing on from the Old Barbary Coast Area, merely walk down Montgomery to the Pyramid at Washington. You are in sight of the east terminus of the world's first operating Cable Car line, which Andrew Hallidie inaugurated in 1873, the original terminus being Clay and Kearny Streets, beside Portsmouth Square.

On the corner of Montgomery and Clay is one of more than 1200 branches of the Bank of America. Apart from its wonderfully restored lobby, this branch office is not, in itself, a significant part of San Francisco's history. But as a portal to the Financial District, nearly any B of A branch will suffice, and so this tangent is in order.

The Bank of America was founded in 1904 as The Bank of Italy by the son of an immigrant couple, Amadeo Peter Giannini. When he took over a small neighborhood bar at the corner of Washington Street and Columbus Avenue, Giannini announced that his was to be a bank for "the little man." Today (1983), with assets exceeding $120 billion, and deposits approaching another $100 billion, it is the largest private banking institution in the world, followed closely by New York's Citicorp.

Before Giannini, banks were intended primarily for wealthy individuals and large businesses. That a maid or a ditch-digger or a small business person could have a savings account, or that he or she might take out a small loan, was not common. The idea of offering complete banking services to ordinary wage earners and the proprietors of small concerns was revolutionary. Despite criticism, scorn, and dire predictions of ruin and doom, Giannini's enterprise had far exceeded his dreams by the time he died in 1949. Later in the day, or at some other time during your visit to The City, you might enjoy taking a look at the Bank's 780-foot-high world headquarters, located on California Street between Montgomery and Kearny. There is a luxurious lounge and restaurant—the Carnelian Room, named after the rare granite that makes up the building's remarkable surface—at the top. It has one of the world's best views, especially at sunset, providing the fog is not in; but be advised that it is one of the few dozen establishments in San Francisco that require jackets and ties of gentlemen, and correspondingly appropriate attire for the ladies.

Montgomery is simply known as "The Street" by local, old-time stock brokers. It is the heart of banking in Western America and looking west across the Pacific Ocean. However, it is not much like New York's Wall Street at all, except that, like its East Coast counterpart, it is rich in history.

The Street was named in honor of Captain John B. Montgomery, the first man to raise the United States flag over San Francisco in 1846. In Montgomery's day, almost all the flat land east and north of where you are standing was under the water of a shallow cove that opened to the Bay. It was around this cove, at Portsmouth Square, one block north of here, that San Francisco really began. Father Junipero Serra's Mission Church, located near Dolores and 16th Streets in what is now called the Mission District, was considered to be way out of town at that time. From a practical standpoint, it had

A view from what is now the area of Montgomery Street near Portsmouth Square in the early 1850's. Where these old ships are in this photo the towers of the Financial District rise today.

very little to do with the actual development of The City.

In the days when water still lapped at the shores of Montgomery Street, of course, it was possible for sailing ships to land here. When the Gold Rush began, the cove—indeed, the entire Bay—became a veritable forest of masts. The ships that anchored here were often abandoned by men whose thoughts had turned from blue water to yellow metal, and many of those abandoned ships were either dismantled to be recycled as building materials, or dragged up into the mud near the cove shore at Portsmouth Square to be converted into hotels, restaurants, brothels, or whatever else could be turned to a profit. These maritime carcasses soon became part of the landfill that virtually covered the cove by the 1870s. Among the most famous of these abandoned ships was the *Niantic,* pulled ashore and converted into a hotel in the earliest days of the Gold Rush and then lost again. In 1978, during excavation for one of the new highrises at the corner of Montgomery and Clay Streets, part of the *Niantic's*

hull resurfaced, preserved in the mud—as you know if you visited the Maritime Museum while you were at Fisherman's Wharf Area (see p. *72*).

By virtue of its location by the cove, ironically, Montgomery Street has been equated with banking and finance, rather than with water, ever since the first fortunes floated down the Sacramento River and into the Bay from the gold fields. From the beginning, the offices of capitalism opened their doors to wealth, and made those doors imposing. The Nevada Bank, which once occupied the corner of Montgomery and Pine Streets, opened on its first day of business with reportedly the largest capitalization of any bank anywhere in the world until that time. Its rental office mantles were constructed of quartz fashioned from the Comstock Lode, and contained such a great amount of gold that at least one early tenant tried to steal them.

Today, as you can see by walking up this street, you can do your San Francisco banking in just about any modern language you desire. From France to Brazil to Japan to China to England to Italy to the Philippines, international banking needs its outposts here.

To begin your tour of the Financial District, walk south down Montgomery Street away from the Old Barbary Coast Area to about center-block past Washington Street near the Pyramid, where Merchant Street runs off to your right toward Chinatown. It was at the intersection of Merchant and Montgomery that the first Pony Express rider arrived here. The Pony Express, of course, was owned by Wells Fargo— about which, more in a moment.

Looking west up Merchant you can see Portsmouth Square at the top, where the alley dead-ends. The Square is much altered from its early days, when it was the political and social center of town. Today it is the major Chinatown park. The Holiday Inn at the top right of the alley, facing the Square, occupies the site where the old Hall of Justice and City Hall used to sit. While the Hall was still standing, one of The City's most famous restaurants, the Blue Fox, opened on Merchant Street. In typical San Francisco style, this extremely high-class eatery advertised itself as being located "just across the street from the Jail." It is still there, as you can see.

Another block down, past Clay Street, I suggest a short side-trip from Montgomery Street up the little alley called Commercial Street. Commerical dates from The City's earliest days, and still has the antique look of the old city. Wells Fargo opened its first office within the half-block just up from Montgomery before coming to fame as proprietor of the Pony Express. The company then moved to the more heavily travelled Montgomery Street presumably as a measure of protection against the hooligans residing in the nearby Barbary Coast.

Wells Fargo, today a major international banking concern with world headquarters at Market and Montgomery, and its short-lived subsidiary, the Pony Express, are by now traditional symbols of heroism, commitment, and bravery as idealized by the Wild West of legend. Wells Fargo was actually founded in New York, by Henry Wells and William Fargo, with the intention of coming to San Francisco. However, once again, the guiding forces behind the company were not really Wells and Fargo at all; the brains belonged to Lloyd Tevis and James Ben Ali Haggin, both of whom became impressive members of The City's millionaire class in short order. Haggin built a large estate on Nob Hill, where the horse stables were so elegant they were the scene of many a fashionable party. Part of Haggin and Tevis's genius consisted in forming the Pony Express.

In the late 1850s and early 1860s, delivery of mail in the West was fabulously slow, difficult, and dangerous. The Pony Express was organized to expedite delivery of financial instruments, as well as love letters and the like. By government contract, Wells Fargo was awarded control of the Overland Mail Co. in 1861, and formed the Trans-Missouri Pony Express, which ran from St. Joseph, Missouri to Sacramento, California. The first Pony Express rider to reach San Francisco arrived here by ferry boat, and galloped up the landing pier to Merchant and Montgomery while observers cheered. Soon, there were other Pony Express branches, not all under Wells Fargo's control. However, this particularly noble experiment involving horse and man came to an unheralded end, its work quickly taken over by the telegraph and the Transcontinental Railroad.*

Involuted as history appears to be, perhaps it will delight you to learn that the Montgomery Street building into which Wells Fargo moved was owned by Sam Brannan, whose name you read in this book's opening chapter as the man who announced, in the streets of San Francisco, the discovery of gold at Sutter's Mill. Brannan was such an extraordinary figure in The City's early days that he is worth something of an aside. Brannan was one of the first Mormons, a church elder and a confederate of Brigham Young himself. As you may know, the original destination of the Latter-Day Saints was generally intended to be California, not what became Salt Lake City, Utah. When the main group of Mormons began their westward trek to the Promised Land, Brannan and about 150 other Saints sailed for San Francisco, still commonly known then as Yerba Buena and not yet part of the United States. Evidently, the plan was for Brannan and his men to establish themselves as a sort of advance guard to pave the way for the rest of the Mormons travelling with Young, and then to create the Mormon empire here. Fortuna had other ideas.

Brannan and his band arrived here in 1847, shortly after Montgomery had raised the American flag at Portsmouth Square. Brannan turned out to be a shrewd, fun-loving gambler, rather than the staid sort of person who is destined to be a successful church elder, and he quickly abandoned the ethereal business of his church for the far more lucrative and pragmatic opportunities at hand, and reportedly absconded with a fair amount of the church's money in the process.

Whatever the case, in his new role as San Francisco's first wheeler-dealer, the generally likeable Brannan soon achieved a reputation for spear heading California firsts. He either

---

*Pony Express rides again! In the spring of 1983, one of the worst winters on record resulted in the closing of the main highway west of Lake Tahoe for weeks by massive landslides. To get the mail through, thirteen horsemen were sworn in as volunteer U.S. mail carriers. The unique event, which made international headlines, was not presided over by Wells Fargo.

intitiated or was the motive force behind the state's first non-Catholic religious service; the first commercial flour mill; the state's first real newspaper, *The California Star;* and the first public school.

He also opened a store in Sacramento, and thereby became a friend of John Sutter's, enabling him to be the messenger of the discovery of gold.

With the Gold Rush, Brannan prospered by selling commodities, newspapers, and real estate, and became The City's first millionaire. When the Barbary Coast got out of hand, Brannan was among the influential San Franciscans who formed the first of the famous vigilante organizations, the Committee of Vigilance, in 1851, which hanged a few of the Coast's rapacious leaders.

Brannan continued to make huge sums of money. He founded such organizations as the Society for California Pioneers, and donated richly to charity and cultural development. But, like so many of The City's early nabobs, his lifestyle primed him for disaster. His businesses started to fail, his real estate deals went bust, he became an alcoholic, and found himself in ruin. Then, in the last year of his life, the Mexican government repaid a large loan he had made to it many years earlier. Immediately, it is said, Brannan reformed. He paid off all his debts and died penniless but happy at the age of seventy.

The City's immense wealth, after 1849, made essential the 1852 order of Congress that a mint be established here, and the first branch office of the United States Mint opened on Commercial Street in 1854. What we now call the Old Mint, located at Mission and Fifth Streets near the Powell and Market Cable Car terminal, opened in 1874 and closed in 1937, when the present Mint, out on Market Street, was opened. The Old Mint is now a government-operated museum, and makes an engaging stop for anyone interested in money and history (see Appendix, p. *157*). If you look east now, from Montgomery Street, you will see that Commercial Street descends toward the Bay to Embarcadero Center, affording a lovely view of the old Ferry Building between the skyscrapers. This vista was thoughtfully planned for, when the first of the Embarcadero highrises started going up. There are a number of good pubs and restaurants along this street, too.

Return to Montgomery Street and proceed south. Along the way you will note several plaques commemorating a few of The City's important people, places and events. San Francisco boasts such a large number of these plaques—many of which are quite proper acknowledgements—that it is a hopeless task to enumerate them. But keep an eye out at about head level when walking about The City, and you will be occasionally greeted by bits of quaint information that will enhance your appreciation and deepen your understanding of the place. Continuing south along Montgomery, you cross Sacramento Street, about at mid-block. You will come to the Wells Fargo Museum, at 420 Montgomery. Its small public area contains a great quantity of memorabilia, including an original Wells Fargo stagecoach, as well as photos, books, records, and other artifacts that make it a stop well worth your while if you have even a passing interest in the early West.

Next, you will come to California Street. In a couple of pages, you will board one of the Cable Cars that runs here for a trip up to Nob Hill; but first, there are a few more sights.

If you look to your right, west up California Street, you will see the imposing carnelian granite and glass Bank of America Building I mentioned at the beginning of this chapter. Across the street, just east on California from where you stand, is the Merchants Exchange Building at 465 California. Walking through its vaulted, sky-lit lobby in the rear will give you some sense of the pomp history has passed on to The City's financial center. If you enjoy this sort of thing, you will find many bank lobbies in this part of town that range from impressive to absolutely gorgeous; indeed, there are far too many to point out here. But the Foundation for San Francisco's Architectural Heritage sponsors a Banking Temples walking tour currently every Thursday at noon, departing from the corner of Clay and Montgomery at the base of the Pyramid, that I am happy to recommend. (See Appendix, p. *166* .) They offer other tours as well.

Walk south on Montgomery one more block to Pine Street and turn left. Across the street, from about mid-block to Sansome, stands the art deco Pacific Stock Exchange Building.

In recent years, with computers making transcontinental connections fast and simple, and with brokers in Los Angeles seeking to consolidate the state's Exchange branches in their territory, the very existence of the Exchange has appeared threatened. But a recognition of its importance has kept it very much alive. You can inquire at the Exchange Office concerning visiting the Exchange Floor.

Across the street from the Stock Exchange, on the south side of the same block as the Merchants Exchange Building, at the corner of Pine and Sansome, is the old Royal Globe Insurance Building—a splendid example of high-rise elegance from the turn of the century. Its marble entryways come from the late Torolonia Palace in Rome. You can get a better look at them from the east side of Sansome Street.

Continue north up Sansome, now, back to California Street. The lobby of the Bank of California, at the northeast intersection of these streets, is one more fine example of the gift of history The City's old bankers have given us; and downstairs is a museum of early Californiana. On California Street, of course, you see the tracks of the California Street Cable Car line. When you're ready, board a Car headed uphill. The slope that rises in the west, where we are headed next, is Nob Hill. You'll pass Grant Avenue/Chinatown on the way (see p. *49*), should you want to stop off there.

In case you're interested in exploring more of the Financial District, let me offer this digression: if you continue south on Montgomery from Pine, you'll see it ends a few blocks down at Market where the Palace Hotel is. Should you be in need of a fine tailor-made suit, head up Pine Street toward Kearny; about half way up the block, near the McDonald's (the only one in the world with a doorman) is the quaint tailor shop of Duncan-Macandrew at 439 Pine (upstairs). The proprietress, Thisby Blake, is a delightful character; the quality of her work is high, the prices low. And, west up Sutter Street from Montgomery, about mid-block, are two architectural de-

lights you should enjoy—the grand Galleria of the new
Crocker Bank Building, and opposite it on Sutter, the Art
Nouveau splendor of the old Hallidie Building. Supposedly,
the Hallidie Building was the first all-glass-front highrise
building; and, yes, it was built by the same man who.
invented the Cable Cars. The Crocker Galleria has several
levels of various businesses, but one deserves special mention: the Ritz Old Poodle Dog restaurant. Founded in 1849,
the Poodle Dog was *the* gastronomic palace of the Nob Hill
crowd during the Golden Era, with a colorful and romantic
history to match; and the current one keeps the tradition
well.

As with Jackson Square/Barbary Coast, my chapter on the
Financial District has been a walking tour, and you are now
familiar with some of the important sights. This is neither a
hotbed of theatre and diversion, nor of shopping—unless
you're buying commodities, stocks, bonds, or options. But,
as you might expect, the Financial District includes some of
The City's outstanding restaurants and bars. While you can
drink at the former, and eat at the latter, their primary
purposes are more distinct here than in most parts of town,
and so I separate the two in listing some of my favorites here.

Restaurants:

The Blue Fox. 659 Merchant Street. 981-1177. ***$$$

The Carnelian Room (top of the Bank of America Building).
555 California Street. 433-7500. **$$$

Le Central. 453 Bush Street. 391-2233. **$$

Orsi. 375 Bush Street. 981-6535. ***$$$

Ritz Old Poodle Dog. 50 Post Street. 392-0353. (Since
1849, the premiere French restaurant in the West.)
**$$$

Tadich Grill. 240 California Street. 391-2373. (Since 1849,
a superb fish house.) ***$$½

Bars:

Harrington's. 245 Front Street. 392-7595.

The London Wine Bar. 415 Sansome Street. 788-4811.

Royal Exchange Saloon. 301 Sacramento Street. 956-1710.

Schroeder's Cafe. 240 Front Street. 421-4778. (Good German food, too.)

Nob Hill

No San Francisco neighborhood is more generously steeped in the extravagent lore of the Golden Era than this opulent little mesa. Because of the outrageous lifestyle that prevailed here from the latter 1870s until 1906, the name Nob Hill still conjures images of a glamorous age when conspicuous consumption, privately-owned business empires richer by far than most nations, and a crassly grand patriotism read themselves into the country's culture as the trappings and symbols of the American Dream.

Living on Nob Hill in the last decades of the nineteenth century was roughly equivalent to living at Fifth Avenue and 57th Street in New York in the same era; only here, instead of Vanderbilt and Whitney, the names were Stanford, Crocker, Huntington, Hopkins—collectively known as the Big Four—and others whom the California bonanza made princes of the West. Early settlers called Nob "The Hill of Golden Promise," because, it is said, on some special evenings the setting sun cast it in a halo of golden light. This celestial display no doubt delighted the hearts of the hordes along Montgomery Street and the old waterfront, and made the Hill an inviting place of escape from the riotous din of the fledgling Gold Rush city below. No one thought of living on this hill in the early days, however, because its slope was too steep, too muddy in winter, and altogether too much of a bother. Eventually one hardy adventuresome soul, a doctor named Hayne, built a modest cottage where the Fairmont Hotel now stands; but he enjoyed his sunsets alone. A few other adventuresome families built modest homes here also, but it was not until the invention of the Cable Car made the Hill's crests easily accessible that living here became practical. Then it became chic, and the Gold Rush millionaires inaugurated a donnybrook of building grand, ornate homes on the south slope, edging up toward heaven from Geary and O'Farrell Streets along Mason, Taylor, and Jones. Hence the name Nob Hill, from nob or nabob.

The first mansions that once adorned this Hill were marvelous, grotesque, romantic. While they were considered to be gross, egocentric displays by some observers, others recognized in them a sincere, if sometimes awkward, attempt to establish a style of culture, while simultaneously patronizing the arts. Palatial mansions are certainly not unique to San Francisco; but the uninhibited splendor of The City's self-made aristocracy resulted in unique attributes in both architectural innovations and attitudes.

The first large mansions belonged to the Eastmans, Tevises, and Hearsts. They were built along Taylor Street, establishing theirs as the most exclusive row of addresses in town. Also on Taylor, at the corner of Clay, James Ben Ali Haggin, the Wells Fargo magnate, built his 60-room extravaganza.

Haggin's palace was soon followed by the first large California Street house, the Tobin mansion, built by the founder of the Hibernia Bank and located where the exclusive Huntington Hotel stands now. Tobin's house established California Street as the choice boulevard of the super-rich, and by the mid-1870s a kind of competition had begun to see who could erect the most extreme version of a residence.

Leland Stanford became the first clear front-runner for these honors when, after becoming governor of the state, he spent some two million 1876 dollars and opened the doors of what was far and away the grandest home in America at that time. Stanford's house contained one of the finest eclectic art collections in the country. His hotel-sized dwelling offered an 18-carat gold and purple velvet sitting room and a large settee in the middle of the main art gallery, in the center of which were large plants whose branches supported gold mechanical birds that reproduced bird songs at the touch of a button. The Chinese government provided the imperial furnishings for the Chinese Room, and there were, in addition, Pompeian, Indian, and other international theme rooms in what sometimes seemed an endless profusion. The mansion stood at the corner of California and Powell Streets — site, today, of the elegant Stanford Court Hotel. But the untimely death of Stanford's 17-year-old son, Leland, Jr., in 1884, made of the place "a great, gloomy barn," as one chronicler of the era reported. In memory of their son, Stanford and his wife, Jane Lathrop Stanford, founded Stanford University on their 9000-acre Palo Alto farm, some 45 miles south of The City.

In constructing his block-square chateau on California between Taylor and Jones Streets, where the beautifully gothic Grace Cathedral now stands, Charles Crocker topped Stanford's extravagence by about a half-million dollars. His family donated the land to the Episcopal Church after the 1906 Quake, but part of the original fence still stands along Taylor and Sacramento Streets. Crocker is reported to have sent his art buyers out with the order to "Give me a million dollars' worth of paintings," and ended up with a veritable museum created by fiat. While this swashbuckling approach to interior decoration had to result in the Crocker home containing at least a few wall hangings that were less than masterful, it also procured a number of genuine finds. Millet's "The Sower" was one of the very few such that were saved when the flames of ought-six swept through the house. Today, the painting hangs in our Palace of the Legion of Honor Museum (see Appendix, p. *157*), a sad and small reminder of the treasures that were lost.

While Crocker was building his domicile, a German undertaker named Yung was living in a small house on a 25-foot lot on the north side of the block Crocker had otherwise bought "entire." Realizing his unique position, Yung demanded an exorbitant price for his property from the building nabob. But Crocker, who had not become wealthy by giving in to pressures of this trifling sort, and who was surely unconcerned about losing a court battle to a member of the hoi polloi, simply enclosed the house and lot of Mr. Yung behind a 45-foot-high wooden fence. Known as the Spite Fence, it became a raging issue in its day symbolizing the division between peasant and plutocrat. After many sunless days Mr. Yung relented and sold his home at what Crocker regarded to be a fair price.

Of all the homes built on Nob Hill during the Golden Era, however, the most fabulous was the gothic monstrosity conceived by Mrs. Mark Hopkins. Erected where the Mark Hopkins Hotel stands today, this three-million-dollar 1880s

fantasy was controversial even among the Hopkins' wealthy peers.

Mark Hopkins himself was a railroad baron of the first water, and much too busy with his enterprises to be concerned about planning and building a large house. He was

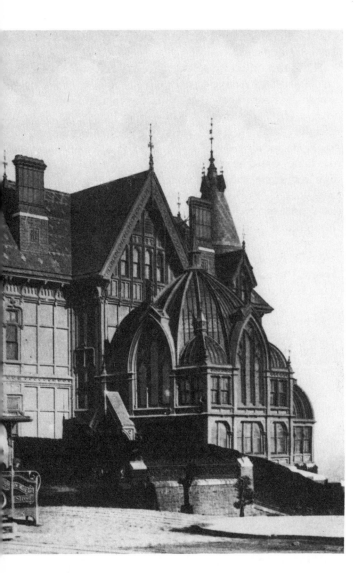

The Mark Hopkins mansion, California & Mason Streets C. 1890.

reportedly conservative, frugal, and indifferent to proving his status with showy displays. In fact, until he died, he lived often in modest quarters he rented downtown for $35 per month. But Mrs. Hopkins, a gold digger 20 years his junior, was Leonine in her desires.

The "lurid imitation of a French castle, combining Gothic and Greek and Arabic and Provincial architecture" was a magnificent parody of all the building that had come before on the Hill. The main dining room sat 60 in baronial splendor. The stone gray towers of the castle (like most of the great mansions here, it was built of wood and painted to look like stone) could be seen from far across the Bay. A 40-foot-high real stone wall surrounded most of the block, and a long, looped, S-shaped driveway led up to the palace from the southwest corner at Pine and Mason Streets, passing through lovely, terraced gardens. The great stone wall and driveway were all that survived the Quake and Fire, and they can still be seen along Pine Street between Mason and Powell; the driveway is used as a business entryway to the Mark Hopkins Hotel.

In her classic tome of pre-Earthquake memoirs, *The Fantastic City,* Amelia Ransome Neville recalled that,

"Within, the house was a mess of anachronisms. One entered portals of a feudal castle to pass into the court of a doge's palace, all carved Italian walnut with a gallery around the second story where murals of Venetian scenes were set between the arches. A beautiful place in itself was this central court, as were many of the individual rooms . . . filled with rare inlaid woods, marble mosaics, and rich furnishings . . . "

Mr. Hopkins died before the house was finished, but he is said to have referred to it (ironically) while it was under construction as the "Hotel de Hopkins." Afterward, Mrs. Hopkins ran off to the East Coast with her architect, and after a scandalous court battle with her estranged son, he inherited the house. It, and its vast art galleries, were subsequently given to the University of California in trust, later to become home of the San Francisco Art Association of the California School of Fine Arts, today known as the San Francisco Art

Institute (see Russian Hill, p. *64*). But, alas, during the 1906 holocaust the palace, with its art treasures and wealth, burned like any shack.

The only Nob Hill mansion to survive the 1906 devastation, in fact, was the imposing brown stone mausoleum built by James "Bonanza Jim" Flood, from Connecticut sandstone, in 1885. Flood had been a Montgomery Street bartender until he cashed in on the Comstock bonanza. It is said he wanted to remind himself of his humble origins, and so he spent $50,000 on a bronze fence surrounding his home. Today the bronze has aged-looking green patina, but in Flood's day a full-time staff of servants was employed to keep it polished. Although Flood's house was gutted by the Big Fire, its superstructure stood. It was restored, and today is the club house of the ultra-exclusive and wealthy Pacific Union Club. Along with the Bohemian Club, the P.U. is a citadel of the West's *old* money and power. Since it is strictly members-only, you are unlikely to have even a glimpse of the opulent restoration undertaken by one of San Francisco's very greatest architects, Willis Polk. But the outside is worth your perusal nonetheless. In case you have trouble seeing it, Flood's monument occupies the entire block on the northwest corner of California and Mason Streets, across from the Fairmont Hotel.

The very top of Nob Hill is still an exclusive neighborhood, but today most of the well-to-do reside in old luxury apartments and posh new condominiums among a few lovely little town houses that were built soon after the Quake. (Today the neighborhoods of Pacific Heights and Sea Cliff are The City's main millionaire districts.) But what dominates the Hill today are not magnificent homes, but grand hotels; and it is with these that any contemporary Nob Hill visitor is likely to be concerned. So I suggest you get off the Cable Car at the intersection of California and Powell Streets, where this line crosses the Powell Street lines, and continue your tour on foot. You will only have to walk one steep block up to Mason; thereafter everything you need to see is on reasonably flat ground. Of course, if need or desire wills it, you can take the California Cable up.

The Stanford Court

The first building at Powell on the southwest side of California Street is The Stanford Court Hotel. Built in 1912 on the site of the old Stanford mansion, it was originally intended to provide luxury apartment accomodations for those Golden Era dowagers who remained in The City. By 1972, however, demand for a new luxury hotel exceeded supply, and after a refurbishment that cost $43,000 per bedroom, this was the answer to the problem. The hotel's old-style elegance is maintained with Baccarat chandeliers, canopied beds, Empire and French Provincial antiques, oak armoires, Carrara marble, stained glass, and extremely gracious service. Fournou's Ovens, the restaurant affiliated with the hotel, is a wonderful spot for dinner; and for a charming interlude, tea is served most afternoons in the hotel's main lobby. It is a "grand lux" hotel in the European tradition.

The Mark Hopkins

At the next corner above you, after you leave The Stanford Court, at Mason, you will arrive at the main entrance to The Mark, as locals know it. Brainchild of a mining engineer turned entrepreneur named George D. Smith, the Mark Hopkins opened its doors in 1926. Although the hotel was named in honor of the Mark Hopkins of railroad fame, and was built on the site of his wife's famous mansion, the Hopkins family has never been associated with it. Smith's inspiration is said to have been New York's Waldorf-Astoria, and he carried out his vision in the grand style of European luxury that was *de rigeur* before the market crashed in 1929, with hand-woven carpets from Austria, rare antique tapestries and murals by famous artists on the walls, hand-carved Spanish furniture, marble patios, and fountains. Smith even persuaded Victor Hirtzler, the world-renowned chef who had made the Hotel St. Francis' kitchens famous, to come out of retirement and take charge of the catering for the hotel's grand opening. This coup helped the Mark to achieve instant success among knowledgeable residents and travellers alike.

The Top of the Mark lounge was another of Smith's inspirations; however, the bar did not open until 1939. Until then, the huge rooms were the penthouse suite of Daniel Jackling, a copper millionaire who was one of the last Golden Era tycoons to live on Nob Hill. He had ordered the unusually high ceilings during the hotel's construction to accommodate the bookshelves required for his massive library. When Jackling retired to a country estate south of The City, Smith turned his suite into what was to become one of the most famous cocktail lounges in the world, where patrons could marvel at the still-unobstructed (1939) view of the Bay, with its two new bridges and the Golden Gate International Exposition being held then on Treasure Island. It is estimated that 30 million people have enjoyed the views and ambience from the Top of the Mark since it opened.

The Mark was a focal point for entertainment and night life during the Big Band Era of the 1940s, with Benny Goodman, Tommy Dorsey, Xavier Cougat, Rudy Vallee, and similar headliners appearing there regularly. The annual New Year's Eve galas were made famous by live radio broadcasts. And The Mark, along with the St. Francis, the Palace, and the Fairmont, was one of the headquarter hotels during the founding of the United Nations in 1945.

The Fairmont

Senator James Fair was the only robber baron who did not build a palatial Nob Hill mansion, although he planned one. He kept a small mansion on the south slope of the Hill, however.

Fair was evidently as unpopular as he was rich. It was reported that he treated employees badly and repossessed the homes of his poorer friends, and forced his own wife into bankruptcy by selling her worthless mining stocks in order to grab her inheritance. She did sue him for divorce in 1883 on the grounds of habitual adultery. But it is also reported that, as a youth in an imperiled wagon train coming West, he became a hero by taking charge and bringing the company safely to California.

Anyway, Tessie Fair, one of James's daughters, inherited the land which her father had acquired from the Porter family, whose modest mansion stood on the site in the 1880s. She employed the Reid Brothers as architects, and construction of the Fairmont began in 1902. As with The Palace and the St. Francis, money was to be no object in the building. Then, just weeks before its grand opening was to take place, the Fairmont met the Earthquake.

The Fairmont was a well-constructed building, and rode out the Quake without suffering too much damage; but the Fire reduced its interior and the crates of opulent furnishings to ashes. An army of workers was put to work restoring the structure almost immediately after the Fire had burned out, and approximately one year following the Quake, the lavish hotel opened its doors in fully restored splendor. The *San Francisco Chronicle* allowed that "there is a magnificent royal palace in Sweden that resembles it on a small scale"; and indeed, with its 400-foot-long, 22-foot-high main room, its marble columns and floors, and its gigantic Florentine mirrors imported from the Castello de Vincigliata, it did look like a palace. And still does.

By location and by design, the Fairmont has become a favorite San Francisco nightspot. Its Cirque Room, recently restored, is an art deco treasure. The Venetian Room is one of The City's most popular supper clubs, which regularly features headline entertainment. The Crown Room, atop the new tower addition, offers grand views as the background to its sumptuous evening meals and Sunday brunch. The outside elevator that takes you to the top has become a celebrated feature. The Brasserie Room serves good food 24 hours a day.

The Huntington Hotel

The Huntington is so exclusive that it really is not much interested in ordinary patronage. People who stay here want their comfort in privacy, and it is the sincerity of the management in protecting its famous, erudite, and wealthy clientele that keeps them coming back—sometimes for stays that last several months.

Erected in the early 1920s by the heirs of C.P. Huntington, and originally called the Huntington Hotel and Apartments, it has always chosen an aura of reserve and relaxed formality. The spacious, comfortable suites are designed for people used to a discreet good life, and are not imposingly lavish. Although the hotel provides its guests with excellent services, you will find nothing out of the ordinary in its lobby except quiet. On either side of its entrance are places you should not miss, however: The Big Four lounge and restaurant (a drink at the bar will transport you back to the Golden Era with real 1890s luxury), and L'Etoile, the favorite French restaurant in San Francisco of the international social elite. It has my favorite piano lounge in the nation, with Peter Mintun at the keyboard.

Other than hotels, the three buildings of greatest interest on Nob Hill today are the Pacific Union Club (of which I have spoken already in connection with James Flood), Grace Cathedral, and the Masonic Hall.

There are several houses of worship in San Francisco that are architecturally stunning; among these are the new St. Mary's Catholic Cathedral at Geary and Gough Streets (near Japantown), the Hebrew Temple Emanu-El at Arguello and Jackson (near Pacific Heights), and the neo-Gothic edifice you see here on Nob Hill, the Episcopal Grace Cathedral, on California and Taylor. Grace Cathedral stands on the site once occupied by the Crocker estate; the land was a gift in the wake of the 1906 Quake and Fire. Although several temporary churches stood here through the 1920s, work on this building did not begin until 1928, and was not finished until 1964. Grace is the third largest Episcopal cathedral in the United States, after the Cathedral of St. John the Divine in New York, and the Cathedral of Saint Peter and Saint Paul in Washington, D.C. Its architecture is largely twelfth and thirteenth century Gothic. Its gilded bronze main doors are exact replicas of the doors in the Baptistry of Florence Cathedral in Italy. They were copies from the originals—the legendary Doors of Paradise, by the fifteenth century master sculptor Lorenzo Ghiberti—made by Bruno Bearsi, and purchased for the Cathedral's 1964 consecration. Guided tours of the Cathedral are conducted Monday through Saturday.

Across the street from Grace Cathedral, the clean-lined white marble structure is Masonic Hall, a monument to and for the order of Freemasons. In addition to the temple and offices, the building houses a 500-car garage, a 3200-seat auditorium, and a large exhibition hall. The auditorium is the scene of frequent concerts and lectures by world-famous performers.

When you've finished your Nob Hill rounds, you might want to catch the Cable along California Street and ride to the west end of the line a few blocks from here. One block before the Cable reaches the end of its line at Van Ness Avenue, it crosses Polk Street, which has become something of a legend in its own time as a major outpost of the modern gay life. (Not, however, *the* outpost, which is located several miles west of the City Center in the Castro district, and is not accessible by Cable Car.) The shopping area some locals refer to as "Polkstrasse" stretches for about a mile from Post Street, four blocks south of the Cable line, north to Union Street; then, after a few short residential blocks, it ends at Ghirardelli Square (see p. 71). The ambience of the walk shifts somewhat from relatively blue-jean-and-punk down around Post, to relatively designer-fashion between Broadway and Union. It is a most heterogeneous street, where sedate Rolls Royces and brash motorcycles share parking meters, and their owners rub elbows shopping, drinking, or dining shoulder to shoulder. There is far too much to do and see along Polk to begin to list here. It is an area best explored by oneself. Most of the bars are gay, but the rest of the street's shops, boutiques and salons are a mixture of everything, from some fine restaurants to antiques, clothes, jewelry and galleries. An adventurous walk on the Polkstrasse will prove worth your while, so please don't let yourself ignore it.

To return downtown, simply take the California Street Cable east back to Chinatown, the Financial District or the Hyatt Regency, or transfer at Powell to your destination of choice along the way.

And now, thank you for joining me on this magical

excursion. In any event, I hope your trip has been as pleasant for you as it has been for me, and that you will visit your favorite parts of The City often; and that, like many others before you, you will leave at least a piece of your heart here in San Francisco. As one of our local poets, Ashley Brilliant, observed, "There may be no heaven anywhere, but somewhere there is a San Francisco."

It will come as no surprise to you to learn that Nob Hill's restaurants are among the best anywhere and among the most expensive in San Francisco. Like some of those in the Union Square and Financial District I mentioned, all these expect gentlemen to wear jackets and ties as well, and the ladies to dress accordingly.

Nob Hill:
Alexis. 1001 California Street. 885-6400. ***$$$
The Big Four (in the Huntington Hotel). 1075 California Street. 771-1140. **$$
Canlis (in the Fairmont). California at Mason. 392-0113. **$$
Fournou's Ovens (in the Stanford Court). 905 California Street. 989-1910. **$$
Le Club. 1250 Jones Street. 771-5400. ***$$$
L'Etoile (in the Huntington Hotel). 1075 California Street. 771-1529. ***$$$
Nob Hill Cafe. 1152 Taylor Street. 776-6915. *$
Nob Hill Restaurant (in the Mark Hopkins). 392-3434. **$$

Polk Street (just a few suggestions to get you started):
Fields Bookstore (famous for metaphysical, occult, rare). 1419 Polk Street. 673-2027.
Le Tournesol (country French cuisine). 1760 Polk Street. 441-1760. **$$
Lord Jim's (an archetypal S.F. fern bar for hetero-singles). Polk and Broadway. 928-3015.
Union Glass Works (art glass). 2235 Polk Street. 673-1105.
Wing Lee (Chinese cuisine). 1810 Polk Street. 775-3210. *$

Appendix A

Some places you may want to visit in San Francisco are located outside the area served by the Cable Cars. While a number of these are far enough away to warrant the use of a taxicab or a rental car, others are just a few blocks from one or more of the Cable lines, and all are accessible by The City's Muncipal Railway System (MUNI). If you want to go from anyplace to someplace else by bus in San Francisco, find out what street you're on and what nearby street intersects it; know the address, street coordinates, or general location of the place you want to reach; then dial 673-6864 (673-MUNI). The operator who answers (you may have to let it ring for awhile) will be able to tell you what bus to take, where to find it, where to transfer if necessary, and where to disembark. Better yet, get a MUNI map, available at the Convention and Visitors Bureau in Hallidie Plaza, and at most hotels and bookstores. Also, there is *A Travelers Map Guide to San Francisco—Sightseeing by Public Transportation* by MOFA; in all major languages. The *Flashmaps—Instant Guide to San Francisco* (including Oakland and Berkeley) is perhaps the best single pocket reference for its comprehensiveness.

In a city the size of San Francisco, hundreds of events occur every day, in hundreds of different locations. Most are listed in our major daily newspapers, some in local magazines, some in neighborhood newsletters, some in handouts posted where passersby may read them. Begin by checking at a newsstand or at your hotel. Natives like to be helpful, so don't be afraid to ask a likely looking local for directions or advice. Obviously, it is impossible in a book of this sort to list every place of importance. What follows is a listing of a few of The City's most prominent, popular, and worthwhile places that I feel will be of interest to a reasonably broad segment of our visitor population. If what you seek is not here, please consult the publications I've indicated above, the telephone directory, and your host or hotel concierge.

CIVIC CENTER. For general reference, the Civic Center is located near the foot of Van Ness Avenue, beginning a couple of blocks north of Market Street. In fact, it spreads out for several blocks north and east of this intersection. The closest you can come by Cable Car is the Market Street depot of the Powell lines, where we began our tour (on p. *26*). From there, walk five long blocks west up Market Street to the United Nations Plaza near Hyde Street. Across the Plaza to the west you will see the imposing dome of City Hall, which is the heart of the Civic Center complex. The Civic Center can also be reached by BART (Civic Center stop), and via MUNI METRO and buses along Market. All Civic Center buildings are open to the public. They include:

San Francisco Museum of Modern Art, housed in the Veteran's Memorial Building. Closed Mondays and major holidays. Admission varies from $1 to $3.50, depending on the principal exhibits. 863-8800 for information.

Louise M. Davies Symphony Hall is home of the San Francisco Symphony Orchestra, and serves a wide variety of concert series and guest performers. Symphony season runs from September until spring. There is a summer season, too. 431-5400.

Opera House is the home for the San Francisco Opera as well as for the San Francisco Ballet Company. Opera season opens in September, ballet in December, various productions throughout the year. 864-3330.

Herbst Theatre, located in the Veteran's Memorial Building, hosts a wide variety of touring and irregular attractions, from lectures to chamber concerts to the Steinway Piano Competition. 431-5400.

Main Library houses not only a trove of books and periodicals, but also lectures, films, and other cultural events—many free of charge. The San Francisco History Room and Archives will offer the curious peripatetic many interesting hours. 558-3981.

Municipal Buildings include the State Building, City Hall, the Public Health Building, and the CIVIC CENTER AUDITORIUM (BROOKS HALL).

YERBA BUENA CENTER is the general redevelopment section that is centered on the George P. Moscone Convention Center. This recent addition to the cityscape is a multipurpose convention and trade show hall with 260,000 square feet of exhibit area and a 28,000 square foot ballroom. It is located two blocks south of Market Street between Third and Fourth Streets, not far from the Palace Hotel. You can make your closest Cable Car approach either from Robert Frost Plaza, at the Hyatt Regency Hotel—the Downtown terminus of the California Street Cable line—or from the Market Street depot of the Powell Street Cable lines, Powell and Market being the closest. From Frost Plaza, walk up Market Street to Third and turn south. From Powell, walk down Market Street to Fourth and turn south. 974-4000.

GOLDEN GATE PARK runs 2½ miles from Stanyan Street, between Fulton and Lincoln Way, west to the Pacific Ocean. In addition to being one of the most lush and lavish urban parks in the world, full of delightful walks and gorgeous vistas, it contains numerous specific places of interest. You cannot reach the park by Cable Car today. Instead, board the #5 MUNI bus at Powell and Market Street going west; disembark at Fulton and 8th Avenue and walk directly into the park. The park's main complex of buildings—constructed around the 1896 World's Fair structures—includes world renowned museums and science halls:

De Young Museum, on the Music Concourse near the east end of the park, exhibits both permanent and touring collections with an emphasis on classic Western art from its European origins. Free tours are available throughout the day, Wednesday-Sunday from 10:00 a.m. until 5:00 p.m. The $2 entry fee also admits you to all other Golden Gate Park museums. 752-5561.

Asian Art Museum, immediately adjacent to the De Young, features more than 10,000 pieces of Asian art, many extremely unusual, including a unique collection of Chinese jade. Open seven days a week from 10:00 a.m. until 5:00 p.m. $2 entry fee, as above. 752-5561.

California Academy of Sciences is located south across the Music Concourse from the De Young. It is open seven days a week from 10:00 a.m. until 5:00 p.m., and there is an entry fee of $1.50 for adults, 75¢ for children. 221-5100 or 221-4214. The Academy is made up of three principal components, which are:

1. *Steinhart Aquarium.* Nearly 200 tanks of fish, ranging from small tropical fish tanks to massive shark enclosures, with a crocodile and turtle pond, simulated tidepools, and a marvelous giant circular fish concourse.

2. *Wattis Hall of Man,* and other science halls. The focus is on human achievements through all cultures and all history.

3. *Morrison Planetarium* features skyshows under a 65-foot-diameter dome, which include the planets, evening skies, and laser light shows. Extra fees, which vary. 752-8268.

Also in the Park:

Japanese Tea Garden. Take green tea and cookies among the birds and plants in exceptionally peaceful surroundings. 75¢, 8:30 a.m. until 4:30 p.m., seven days.

Stowe Lake Boat House. Rent a rowboat by the hour and cruise leisurely in this doughnut-shaped lake around a central island ideal for easy hiking.

Conservatory. A magnificent Victorian glass palace of permanent plants and a changing exhibition of flowers in season. Seven days, 10:00 a.m. until 5:00 p.m. 558-4916.
Strybing Arboretum. An open-air park within a park full of botanical delights. 558-3622.

MARINA and the GOLDEN GATE NATIONAL RE-CREATION AREA now has as its center a converted group of antiquated military structures centered at Fort Mason, on the water, with a stunning view of the Golden Gate. The GGNRA's park lands include much of western Marin County, as well as this end of The City. The offerings in Fort Mason itself include theatres, a music school, the celebrated Greens Restaurant, and the offices for many of San Francisco's creative guilds, such as the Graphic Arts Guild and the Media Alliance. 441-5705.

Palace of Fine Arts/Exploratorium. Designed by Bernard Maybeck for the 1915 World's Fair, and the only one of that exposition's structures extant, the Palace is the setting for such major San Francisco events as the annual Film Festival; but its grounds and architecture are worth a visit any time. The world-famous Exploratorium is a unique museum of human perception—a science museum dedicated to the art of discovery where you play with the exhibits, which are really educational toys for adults as well as for children. $2.50 for adults 18 or older. Take the #30 MUNI bus north through the tunnel to the Marina District from Stockton and Sutter, one block northeast of Union Square. Board near the east side tunnel. This bus goes through Chinatown, North Beach and the Wharf Area on its route. Wednesday, Thursday, and Friday, 1:00-5:00 p.m.; Saturday and Sunday, 11:00 a.m.-5:00 p.m.

Golden Gate Promenade. A walk along the secluded waterfront to Fort Point, underneath the Golden Gate Bridge. Fort Point itself—a marvelous Civil War-era military fortress, now restored—can be reached by the #28 MUNI bus from

Bay and Laguna Streets at Fort Mason. Seven days from
10:00 a.m. until 5:00 p.m.
556-2857.

Palace of the Legion of Honor houses a collection of art emph-
asizing French contributions, but exhibiting international
masters new and old. A copy of the original in Paris and a gift
of the Spreckles family, it is located in the northwest corner
of The City in Lincoln Park, commanding a peerless view of
the Golden Gate. #2 MUNI bus on Sutter Street, one block
north of Union Square. Wednesday-Sunday, 10:00 a.m.-
5:00 p.m. $2 admission will also let you into the museums in
Golden Gate Park, if you go on the same day.

Coit Tower has been discussed earlier in this book (see p. 85),
but is worth a separate mention here. You can find a spectacular view of The City and environs from the top of
Telegraph Hill. Parking is available but very crowded most
of the day. #39 MUNI bus chugs its way up the hill as well,
from Fisherman's Wharf near Aquatic (Victorian) Park. 75¢
to take the elevator to the top.

San Francisco Zoo, in a pleasant, park-like setting far to The
City's south side, and west almost to the ocean. The L-Metro
subway car from the Powell Street MUNI station (call 673-
MUNI). Seven days, 10:00 a.m. until 5:00 p.m. Adults,
$2.50.

Old Mint, Fifth and Mission Streets, is only one block south
of the Market-Powell Street Cable Car depot, and an easy
walk from the Financial District or Union Square. This
building survived 1906 and is full of historic exhibits, including $1 million in gold display. 974-0783.

Golden Gate Bridge. Golden Gate Transit bus service will take
you across the Bridge. 332-6600. If driving from downtown, take Van Ness Avenue (Highway 101 North) to
Lombard and follow the signs. The Bridge administrative
offices: 921-5858.

Appendix B

If you have a car and some time to play, you will find that one of San Francisco's charms is its ready access to unusual things to see and do in the surrounding communities. If you ski and/or gamble, you are about four hours by car (or one by air) from Reno and Lake Tahoe, on the California/Nevada border. If you scuba dive, you are about two-and-one-half hours by car from Monterey Bay to the south, or the Mendocino County coast to the north. Between these extremes lie many less strenuous excursions.

Muir Woods is part of the land protected by the Golden Gate National Recreation Area in Marin County. Although the tallest of the giant redwoods are much farther north, this park gives a very good sense of the grandeur of a true redwood forest. If you don't want to take the drive by car, four tour companies go from San Francisco to Muir Woods and back daily, usually with a stop in the picturesque Marin town of Sausalito. They are:

Dolphin Tours: 441-6853

Gray Line Tours: 771-4000

Great Pacific Tour Company: 929-1700

Lorrie's Travel and Tours: 885-6060

Wine Country. Although some will debate the proper rankings, Northern California's wine country has proved itself at least competitive with its peers in France, Germany, Spain, and Italy; and usually its high quality comes at a moderate price. Some of the world's finest grapes become some of the world's finest wines, only an hour or two north from San Francisco. If you want to spend a few days exploring by car, there are numerous country inns, hotels, and motels in the region where you can rest comfortably between stops. (Most bookstores downtown have guides to their romantic offerings.) Otherwise, all the tour companies listed above for

Muir Woods sponsor wine country tours; so does California Pacific Coast Tours, at 362-8800. Tasting rooms are frequent, and a special guide to the wineries is recommended. There are also a few major wineries to the south of The City. The tour companies listed herein also offer tours of the wine country.

Yosemite National Park, one of America's greatest natural wonders, is only five hours southeast of The City by car. Take Highway 580 to Highway 205 to Highway 120. The various tour companies listed herein also offer tours.

Monterey and Carmel. The grandeur of the California coast at its best. Monterey was, for many years, a great fishing and fish canning town, made famous by John Steinbeck. It is now a gracious city with a nostalgic waterfront, where one of the world's great aquariums is being constructed. Carmel, known as a resort town in the best sense of the word, is farther down Highway 1 just a few miles or take the famous "17-mile Drive." About a three-hour drive south from The City. The tour companies listed herein also offer tours of Monterey and Carmel.

The Bay is a tour you can take in a single day, virtually any day, with narration. Or you can simply join the commuters ferrying to various points in Marin County.

Red and Gold Fleet: 781-7877
Red and White Fleet: 546-2803
Hornblower Yachts (parties on the water): 540-8332
Golden Gate Ferry Service (to Sausalito and Larkspur): 332-6600
Tiburon Ferry: 546-2815

Alcatraz Tours. Dock-to-dock, this two-hour visit to the long-off-limits former Federal prison carries a ferry fee from Pier 43. $2 adults, $1 children. 556-0560 or 546-2805 or 556-4122.

Angel Island Bring walking shoes and a picnic lunch, because there are no services on this 640-acre nature preserve. Ferries daily in summer, weekends in winter. $5.25 adults, $2.75 children. 435-1915 or 546-2815.

Oakland. There is a lot there, and much of it well worth seeing—the mansions of the Piedmont District are marvelous, and the size of the port, San Francisco's nemesis . . .

City of Oakland offices. 654-6161.

Chamber of Commerce. 451-7800.

Oakland Tours Program. 273-3234.

Oakland Museum. 273-3402 or 273-3514 (tours).

Oakland Symphony. 465-6400.

Oakland Ballet. 530-0447.

Oakland International Airport. 444-4444.

Paramount Theatre (an art deco splendor). 465-6400.

Oakland Convention and Visitors Bureau. 763-4574.

Berkeley. A walk down Telegraph Avenue and through the campus should not be missed . . .

University of California. 642-6000.

Lawrence Hall of Science Museum. 642-5132.

Art Museum. 642-0808.

Mayor's Office. 644-6484.

Stanford University (Palo Alto—Menlo Park).

Tours and information. 497-2053.

Palo Alto City Hall. 329-2311.

Other information. 497-2300.

Stanford Research Institute (SRI). 326-6200.

Art Museum. 497-4177.

Appendix C

A number of areas mentioned in this book are subjects of guided tours offered by organizations with particular interest in, and knowledge of, each section. Among them:

Gold Rush City. A walking tour of the historical Jackson Square/Barbary Coast area (see pp. *120-128*). First and third Wednesdays of the month, 12:00 noon. Departs from the Clay Street lobby of the Transamerica Pyramid, 600 Montgomery Street. Free, no reservations required. Friends of the San Francisco Public Libary. 558-3770.

Historic Market Street. A walking tour (see pp. *97-109*). First and third Tuesdays of the month, 2:00 p.m. Departs from One Market Plaza at the very foot of Market Street. Free, no reservations required. Friends of the San Francisco Public Library. 558-3770.

North Beach. A walking tour stressing culture past and present (see pp. *81-95*). Every Saturday, 10:00 a.m. Departs from the steps of Sts. Peter and Paul Cathedral, 666 Filbert Street, across from Washington Square Park. Free, no reservations required. Friends of the San Francisco Public Libarary. 558-3770.

Chinatown. (See pp. *49-61* .) The Culinary Walk requires advance reservations; the $12 fee includes lunch. 986-1822. The Heritage Walk emphasizes history and culture, and begins Saturdays at 2:00 p.m. at a cost of $6 adults, and $2 children. 986-1822. Ding How Walking Tours does Chinatown at night. 981-8399.

Fisherman's Wharf. (See pp. *67-77* .) Carriage Charter provides a romantic, horse-drawn carriage tour. 398-0857.

Civic Center. A walking tour concentrating on history and the grand architecture of local government buildings. Every Thursday at 12:00 noon. Departs from the San Francisco Room, 3rd floor, Main Library, 200 Larkin Street in the Civic Center. Free. Friends of the San Francisco Public Library. 558-3770.

Coit Tower. (See pp. *85-88*.) The tour emphasizes the controversial tower murals. Every Saturday at 11:00 a.m. Departs from the reception desk of the tower. Free. Friends of the San Francisco Public Library. 558-3770.

Moscone Center. The focus is on architecture, historical and modern, in the Yerba Buena Center area. Saturdays at 1:00 p.m. Departs from the Moscone Center front door, Howard Street between Third and Fourth Streets. Free. Friends of the San Francisco Public Library. 558-3770.

Pacific Heights Victorians. A walking tour through a neighborhood of attractive and often luxurious mansions, most of which were built in the late 19th century. Recently, some of these homes have sold for millions each. Twice on Saturdays, at 10:00 a.m. and 2:00 p.m. Departs from Mary Ellen Pleasant Park, Bush and Octavia Streets. Free. Friends of the San Francisco Public Library. 558-3770.

Presidio Army Museum. Saturday and Sunday, 1:00 p.m. Departs from Building #1, Lincoln and Funston Streets in the U.S. Army Base Presidio. Free. Call 561-2211 for more information.

Golden Gate Park. Various walking tours between May and October. Except as noted, free. 221-1310.

> *East End.* Sundays at 11:00 a.m. Meet in front of Park Directory at the Academy of Sciences.
> *Japanese Tea Garden.* Sundays at 2:00 and 3:00 p.m. Meet inside front gate of garden. 75¢ admission.

Strawberry Hill. Saturdays at 2:00 p.m. Meet in front of Japanese Tea Garden.

West End. Saturdays at 2:00 p.m. Meet in front of Park Directory near buffalo paddocks.

Strybing Arboretum. Various walks. 661-0822.

Dashiell Hammett Tour. Visit the locations mentioned in the classic Sam Spade novels. Sundays at 12:00 noon. Departs from in front of the Main Library, Larkin at McAllister. $4, adults. 564-7021.

Special City Tours (including tours of the greater Bay Area). In the San Francisco tradition, these tours might be seen as many different strokes for many different folks. Each tour operator provides his or her special perspective, and specifics of the tours may change; hence, this listing can offer only minimal information.

Cappa and Graham. 239-1934 (group and convention service).

San Francisco Connection, Ltd/San Francisco Walking Tours. 788-8822 (custom tours and services).

San Francisco Tour Representative Services. 398-6089 (tours and ground operations)

Tour Escort Services: 956-2960. (custom tours and guides)

Gray Line. 771-4000.

San Francisco by air:

Helicop-Tours. 495-3333.

Commodore Helicopters. 981-4832.

San Francisco by 70-foot schooner: 431-4590. From Pier 39 (summer only).

San Francisco for Children, and other custom tours: 392-5660. Also, *Places to Go with Children in Northern California,* by Elizabeth Pomada, is a good book.

San Francisco Theatre: Not so much tour information, as information about everything theatrical, including a fine theatrical library.

Theatre Communications Center of the Bay Area, 2940 16th Street, Room 102, San Francisco, CA 94103. 621-0427.

Sailing Charters. 221-3333.
Fishing Trips and Charters. 673-9815.
Marine World-Africa U.S.A. 591-7676.

Appendix D

USEFUL TELEPHONE NUMBERS

Police, Fire, Emergency: dial 911.
San Francisco General Hospital, 1001 Potrero Avenue.
821-8200.

Public Transportation:

Covers entire city:
San Francisco Municipal Railway (MUNI). 673-6864 (673-MUNI).
Subway to Berkeley and Oakland in East Bay:
Bay Area Rapid Transit (BART). 788-2278.
Covers East Bay Cities; Berkeley; Oakland, etc:
AC Transit. 653-3535.

Covers Palo Alto and San Jose:
SAM-TRANS. 761-7000.
Covers Marin County Cities; Sausalito, San Rafael, etc.:
Golden Gate Transit. 322-6600.
Airport bus service: 673-2432 for information. 24-hour service to San Francisco International and Oakland International from Downtown San Francisco pick up at major hotels in The City.

Sports:

San Francisco Giants. 467-8000.
San Francisco 49ers. 468-2249.
Oakland A's. 638-0500.

Taxicabs:

DeSoto Cab. 673-1414.
Luxor Cab. 552-4040.

Veteran's Cab. 532-1300.
Yellow Cab. 626-2345.
For other taxicab listings, see phone book.

Limousine Services:

Associated Limousines and Tours. 563-1000.
Ishi Limousine. 567-4700.
Nob Hill Limousine and Tours. 585-7500.
Tri-Terminal Limousine Service and Tours. 467-8268.
For other limousine listings, see phone book.

Major San Francisco Art Museums and Other Exhibitions:

Asian Art Museum. 558-2993.
California Academy of Sciences. 752-8268.
California Palace of the Legion of Honor. 558-2881.
M.H. De Young Memorial Museum. 558-2887.
Exploratorium (at the Palace of Fine Arts). 563-3200.
National Maritime Museum. 556-8177.
San Francisco Museum of Modern Art. 863-8800.

Miscellaneous:

San Francisco Zoo. 661-4844.
San Francisco Main Library. 558-3191.
Foundation for San Francisco's Architectural Heritage. 441-3000.
San Francisco Symphony/Louise M. Davies Symphony Hall. 431-5400.
San Francisco Opera House. 431-5400.
San Francisco Ballet. 621-3838.
Performing Arts Center Tours. 552-8338.
San Francisco Convention and Visitors Bureau. 626-5500, 974-6900 or 391-2000.
San Francisco Chamber of Commerce. 392-4511.
San Francisco's Mayor's Office. 558-3456 or 558-2666.

San Francisco City Hall. 558-6161.

San Francisco International Airport. 761-0800.

Gay Events Information (tape). 861-1100.

Cable Car Museum (at the Cable Car Barn). 474-1887.

Fort Mason Cultural Center. 441-5705.

Chinese Historical Society. 391-1188.

Japantown Center. 922-6776, 346-3243.

Italian Museum. 398-2660.

San Francisco African-American Historical and Cultural Society. (Fort Mason Center.) 441-0640.

Mexican Museum. (Fort Mason Center.) 441-0404.

American Youth Hostels. (Fort Mason Center.) 771-4646.

Some Major Stage Theatres:

Alcazar Theatre. 775-7100.

American Conservatory Theatre. 771-3800.

Curran Theatre. 673-4400.

Fugazi (Beach Blanket Babylon). 421-4222.

Geary Theatre. 673-6440.

Golden Gate Theatre. 775-8800.

Intersection. 982-2356.

Lamplighters Music Theatre. 752-7755.

Magic Theatre. 441-8822.

Marines Memorial Theatre. 673-6440.

Music Hall Theatre. 776-8996.

On Broadway. 398-0800.

Orpheum. 474-3800.

Theatre on the Square. 433-9300.

Some Downtown S.F. Night Clubs and Other Live Entertainment:

Studio West (S.F.'s answer to New York's Studio 54 disco). 781-6357.

The Plush Room Cabaret. 885-6800.

The Venetian Room (Fairmont Hotel). Live name entertainment. 772-5163.

The Punch Line. Live name entertainment. 474-3801.

The Warfield Theatre. 775-7722.

Great American Music Hall (name entertainment). 885-0750.

Turk Murphy's Earthquake McGoon's (Dixieland jazz). 986-1433.

Wolfgang's (live name entertainment; formerly The Boarding House and Old Waldorf). 441-4333.

Starlight Roof (Sir Francis Drake Hotel). Dancing. 392-7755.

The Oz (in the St. Francis tower). High fashion disco. 397-7000.

Masonic Auditorium. 776-4917.

Kimball's (name jazz). 861-5555.

Silhouettes. ('50's Rock and Roll). 398-1952.

Major Downtown Hotels:

Quick phone reference:
Clift. 775-4700.
Fairmont. 772-5000.
Hilton. 771-1400.
Hyatt Regency. 788-1234.
Hyatt Union Sq. 398-1234.
Mark Hopkins. 392-3434.
Méridien. 974-6400.
Palace. 392-8600.
St. Francis. 397-7000.
Sir Francis Drake. 392-7755.
Stanford Court. 989-3500.

Unusual Hotels:

Check the "Bed and Breakfast Inns" listings in the S.F. phone book yellow pages under "Hotels." Also, call the Mansion Hotel. 929-9444.

Tickets (all events and shows):

Ticketron. 495-4088.

Bay Area Seating Service (BASS). 835-3849.

Appendix E

SELECTED BIBLIOGRAPHY and SUGGESTIONS FOR
FURTHER READING

Aidala, Thomas, and Curt Bruce. *The Great Houses of San Francisco*. New York: Alfred Knopf, 1974.

Asbury, Herbert. *The Barbary Coast*. New York: Alfred Knopf, first ed. 1933. (The definitive work on this subject.)

Baum, Hank (ed.). *The San Francisco Art Review: An Art Explorer's Guide*. Chicago: The Krantz Co., 1981.

Becker, Howard S. (ed.), *Culture and Civility in San Francisco*. New Jersey: Transaction Books, 1972.

Beebe, Lucius, and Charles Clegg. *San Francisco's Golden Era*. Berkeley: Howell-North, 1960. (Plus other works by these authors.)

Bronson, William. *The Earth Shook, The Sky Burned*. Garden City: Doubleday and Co., 1959.

Caen, Herb. *Bhagdad By the Bay*. Garden City: Doubleday and Co., 1949. (Plus other works by this author.)

Cook, Bruce. *The Beat Generation*. New York: Charles Scribner's Sons, 1971.

Delehantz, Randolph. *Walks and Tours in the Golden Gate City*. New York: The Dial Press, 1980.

Dickson, Samuel. *San Francisco is Your Home* (1947); *San Francisco Kaleidoscope* (1949); *The Streets of San Francisco* (1955). Palo Alto: Stanford University Press.

Doss, Margot Patterson. *San Francisco At Your Feet*. New York: Random House, 1974. (Plus other works by this author.)

Edwords, Clarence E. *Bohemian San Francisco*. 1914 classic. Berkeley: Silhouette Press, reprint edition, 1973.

Ferlinghetti, Lawrence, and Nancy J. Peters. *Literary San Francisco*. New York: Harper & Row, 1980.

Gentry, Curt. *The Madams of San Francisco*. New York: Ballantine Books, 1964.

Hansen, Gladys, S.F. City Archivist. *San Francisco Almanac*. San Rafael, Ca: Presidio Press, 1980. (Plus other works by this author.)

Hirzler, Victor. *The Hotel St. Francis Cookbook*. Chicago: The Hotel Monthly Press, 1919.

Hoover, F. Herbert. *Hoover's Guide to Galleries: San Francisco*. Los Angeles: Camaro Publishing Col, 1974.

Hunt, Rockwell. *Stories of the States: California the Golden*. Silver, Burdett & Co., 1911.

Irwin, Will. *The City that Was*. New York: Huebsch, 1906.

Jackson, Joseph Henry (ed.). *The Western Gate: A San Francisco Reader*. New York: Farrar, Straus & Young, 1952.

Kahn, Edgar M. *Cable Car Days in San Francisco*. Palo Alto: Stanford University Press, 1966.

Lewis, Oscar. *Bay Window Bohemia*. Garden City: Doubleday & Co., 1956. (Plus other works by this author.)

Lewis, Oscar. *San Francisco: Mission to Metropolis*. Berkeley: Howell-North, 1966.

Myrich, David P. *San Francisco's Telegraph Hill*. Berkeley: Howell-North, 1972.

Neville, Amelia Ransome. *The Fantastic City*. Cambridge: Houghton Mifflin Co., The Riverside Press, 1932.

Olmsted, R., and T. H. Watkins, for the Junior League of San Francisco. *Here Today: San Francisco's Architectural Heritage*. San Francisco: Chronicle Books, 1978.

San Francisco Bay Guardian (eds.). *San Francisco Free and Easy*. San Francisco: Headlands Press, 1980.

Thomas, Gordon, and Max M. Witts. *The San Francisco Earthquake*. New York: Stein & Day, 1971.

Van der Zee, John, and Boyd Jacobson. *The Imagined City*. San Francisco: California Living Books, 1980.

Watkins, T.H., and R. Olmstead. *Mirror of the Dream*. San Francisco: Scrimshaw Press, 1976. (The best current single- volume history of The City.)

Wells, Evelyn. *Champagne Days of San Francisco*. New York: Appleton-Century, 1943.

Woodbridge, John and Sally Woodbridge. *Architecture San Francisco*. San Francisco: 101 Productions, 1982.